START AND RUN A

Delicatessen

Visit our How To website at **www.howto.co.uk**

At **www.howto.co.uk** you can engage in conversation with our authors – all of whom have 'been there and done that' in their specialist fields. You can get access to special offers and additional content but most importantly you will be able to engage with, and become a part of, a wide and growing community of people just like yourself.

At **www.howto.co.uk** you'll be able to talk and share tips with people who have similar interests and are facing similar challenges in their lives. People who, just like you, have the desire to change their lives for the better – be it through moving to a new country, starting a new business, growing their own vegetables, or writing a novel.

At **www.howto.co.uk** you'll find the support and encouragement you need to help make your aspirations a reality.

You can go direct to **www.start-and-run-a-delicatessen.co.uk** which is part of the main How To site.

How To Books strives to present authentic, inspiring, practical information in their books. Now, when you buy a title from **How To Books,** you get even more than just words on a page.

START AND RUN A

Delicatessen

Deborah Penrith

howtobooks / **smallbusinessstart-ups**

The paper used for this book is FSC certified and totally chlorine free. FSC (The Forest Stewardship Council) is an international network to promote responsible management of the world's forests.

Published by How To Books Ltd,
Spring Hill House, Spring Hill Road,
Begbroke, Oxford OX5 1RX, United Kingdom
Tel: (01865) 375794 Fax: (01865) 379162
info@howtobooks.co.uk
www.howtobooks.co.uk

How To Books greatly reduce the carbon footprint of their books by sourcing their typesetting and printing in the UK.

British Library Cataloguing in Publication Data.
A catalogue record for this book is available from the British Library.

ISBN 978 1 84528 314 8

Produced for How To Books by Deer Park Productions, Tavistock
Typeset by PDQ Typesetting, Newcastle-under-Lyme, Staffordshire
Printed and bound in Great Britain by Cromwell Press Group, Trowbridge, Wiltshire

NOTE: The material contained in this book is set out in good faith for general guidance and no liability can be accepted for loss or expense incurred as a result of relying in particular circumstances on statements made in the book. Laws and regulations are complex and liable to change, and readers should check the current position with the relevant authorities before making personal arrangements.

CONTENTS

PREFACE

Food and beverages are essential and affect each and every one of us, they are literally our lifeblood. If you're thinking about starting a delicatessen, there is always a way to make it happen and now might be the right time to transform that dream of being your own boss into a reality. Be heartened by the fact that start-up facts and figures are very encouraging. More than half a million people in the UK start their own business each year and, contrary to popular belief, more than 80% of small businesses are still going strong 12 months after starting up.

Says Bob Farrand, Managing Director of The Guild of Fine Food:

> *The business end of the delicatessen equation is substantially similar to the opening of most other food retail operations. Factors such as footfall, competition, refurbishment, start-up and staffing costs, stock reductions, and promotion all need to be examined as part of the overall business plan. However, the key to success also rests with in-depth product knowledge – selecting the best and knowing why it is best – and communicating this to your customers.*

The fine food retailing sector plays a vital role in the UK economy and with tastes becoming more and more exotic and diverse, this means as a deli owner you need to take account of new developments and changes in people's attitudes. The information and guidance in this book have been collated from a selection of hands-on deli owners and other business and industry sources and should give you the details and tools to start out. Hopefully, it will guide you through the ups and downs and once you have digested it all, don't be disheartened by the apparent bureaucratic red tape. It is not really that overwhelming and in the words of Angus Ferguson, Managing Director of Demijohn deli in Edinburgh and Glasgow: 'As long as you know what you will eventually need to do to fulfil all the legal requirements for being in business, just get started.'

It's time to put all your wonderful new ideas into practice. These, together with a willingness and passion to learn and respond to new trends and tastes, should put your foot further on the ladder to success in this exciting and challenging business.

1

A WORLD IN ONE SHOP

People's tastes have become more sophisticated, diverse and adventurous over the past 20 years and the popularity of delicatessens, speciality and fine foods has grown by leaps and bounds. Italian, Jewish, German and Polish delicatessens have sprouted virtually overnight to cater for expanding immigrant communities in the UK. From their early faltering days they have blossomed as their customer base has changed to include that sector of the British population who are keen to sample food and drink tasted abroad or in local continental and Asian restaurants.

The word delicatessen is arguably the most well-known foreign word in the English language. It entered into English usage from the German *delikatessen* (the plural of the French *delicatesse*) meaning a 'delicacy' and *essen* 'to eat.' The word *delicate* is recorded in Spanish as *delicatus*, meaning 'giving pleasure, delightful.'

Usually a delicatessen is simply referred to as a deli. It sells fresh produce, including meats, cheeses and juices and stocks other products such as confectionery, cereals and pasta, bread, pickles and preserves, condiments and sauces, imported goods and related items such as cookbooks, cooking oils, and utensils. A number have also expanded to offer eating areas and to prepare sandwiches, salads and drinks to order.

With consumer tastes becoming more cosmopolitan, and delicatessens largely catering to them, supermarkets, convenience stores and other food retailers have not been slow to open in-store deli counters, expanding their ranges of cheeses, patés, olives and dips and introducing Polish, continental and Far Eastern food and drink.

Says Fi Buchanan, of Heart Buchanan Fine Food & Wine in Glasgow: 'Supermarkets are taking their lead from delis and more and more the word deli is being ascribed to the higher end lines in supermarkets. Keep a keen eye on all developments and learn from them. Delis are not generic but something much more personal, providing a service to your local community.'

Now that you have decided to open a deli, take a look at all the complementary services you can offer to take advantage of your specialist, niche market. Remember that consumer needs are changing all the time so keep evolving your business to stay ahead of your competitors.

The national banking group the Alliance & Leicester suggests you consider the following before starting out:

☐ Who your customers will be – you might look at targeting the catering trade as well as members of the public.

☐ Where your premises will be – a good location is very important.

☐ Whether you will have more than one outlet, for example a market stall as well as a shop.

☐ Whether you will have an internet presence and take orders online.

☐ Whether you will offer a delivery service.

☐ What your opening hours will be.

☐ What range of products you will stock.

☐ Where you will obtain your stock from.

☐ Whether you will make up any dishes yourself, such as pâtés.

☐ Whether you will apply for a licence to sell alcohol.

☐ Whether you will offer organic products.

☐ Whether you will offer a range of Fairtrade products.

☐ How you will monitor which are popular/unpopular lines.

☐ Whether you will serve take-away food (such as sandwiches and bagels) for the lunch-time and after-work trade.

☐ Whether you should set up an in-store café as well, offering pastries and fresh coffee to have in or take-away, as well as a mail order/internet hamper service.

☐ Whether you can extend to catering for private and business functions.

☐ What your pricing policy will be (don't forget you must be able to cover your costs, overheads and drawings).

☐ How you will set your prices and how frequently you will review them.

☐ Whether you will offer credit and, if so, to whom.

☐ Whether you will offer discounts, special offers and so on.

Hopefully you will find an answer to these within the pages of this book.

Making an impact

Around half a million people take the plunge and start up their own business each year and there are more than 4.3 million small businesses in total in the UK. Of these, 2.72 million are sole proprietors. Small and medium-sized enterprises (SMEs) employ 12 million people, or 58% of the private sector workforce, and turnover totals £1.2 billion, which is 50% of the UK's gross domestic product.

Says Britain's Prime Minister Gordon Brown: 'Small businesses are at the forefront of the innovation and enterprise that is the foundation of our economic success. I am continuously impressed by the countless small businesses which represent these very qualities.' Adds David Cameron, leader of the Conservative Party: 'Small businesses are the lifeblood of the British economy and their success is vital if we are to succeed in the 21st century.'

'Small businesses form a vital part of the current government's ambitious growth agenda and help create a dynamic and growth-driven economy,' says the Federation of Small Businesses (FSB). However, while there is this recognition of the small business sector's importance, small businesses do continue to face difficulties in a number of key areas and it is important to know what problem areas you might face.

The Department for Business, Enterprise & Regulatory Reform (BERR) broadly rates the following as obstacles to business success:

☐ Competition in the market – 15%

☐ Regulations – 14%

☐ Taxation, VAT, PAYE, National Insurance, business rates – 12%

☐ The economy – 10%

☐ Cash flow – 10%

☐ Recruiting – 6%

☐ Shortage of skills generally – 4%

- ☐ Availability/cost of suitable premises – 4%

- ☐ Obtaining finance – 3%

- ☐ No obstacles – 2%

- ☐ Shortage of managerial skills/expertise – 1%

It's interesting to note that, contrary to what you might expect, raising the necessary cash is far from being the major obstacle you will face. That distinction is reserved for facing up to competition in the marketplace.

Establishing economic resilience

A record 471,500 new businesses opened their doors in 2007 – the highest annual volume since Barclays Bank started tracking the market in 1988 – in spite of increasingly difficult trading conditions in the second half of that year. Slower economic growth is indeed likely to curtail the buoyancy of start ups but John David, Marketing Director for Barclays Local Business, still expects the small business sector to prove resilient.

Deloitte has warned that the UK economy is set to experience its weakest period of growth in 15 years and that there is a risk of a recession in the next two years. The UK economy was expected to grow by 2% in 2008 and by a slightly smaller margin in 2009. According to George Derbyshire, Managing Director of the National Federation of Enterprise Agencies (NFEA), there could still be a continued growth in small businesses despite a downturn in the markets.

‘There is no question that the economy as a whole is facing a difficult time as a result of substantial increases in many input costs, particularly fuel, energy and food, together with pressures in the financial markets. However, I believe that the greatest danger is that we talk ourselves into recession. Confidence is a fragile flower and public commentators have a duty to be balanced in their comments and to reflect on the consequences of their statements.

The general mood of SMEs in this economic climate is of concern, not helped by some of the comments they are hearing and reading about from commentators. At the same time, a number of businesses are expressing confidence in their markets and indeed their own management ability. Small business owners are renowned for their resourcefulness, resilience and optimism - traits which will stand them in good stead at present.

... and of course, SMEs should be aware that business support services, such as those available from local enterprise agencies, can help in a number of ways. They can review and advise on business plans and provide training on specific skills, such as credit control, negotiating, marketing and selling for instance. They can also advise clients with strained cash flows how to raise, and indeed manage without, new funding.

Your projected performance is thus subject to a myriad of factors, from overall economic trends to pressure from competitors. You need to keep customers loyal and deliver compelling offers. While you are strategising for a slow-down in the market, quality may come under the spotlight, but quality is an important differentiator at all times and will help to keep you ahead of your rivals.

The Guild of Fine Food's recent survey found that delis are better able to weather changing economic and competitive conditions than many other businesses. While some consumers may cut back on the number of times they eat out, or spend less when they do go out, one of the best ways to overcome this is to offer your customers opportunities that will establish and deepen their loyalty. When the good times return you are thus more likely to emerge as a winner by having created a close and lasting bond with your customers during more difficult times.

Says Angus Ferguson, Managing Director of Demijohn deli in Edinburgh and Glasgow:

We are busier now than at any moment in our short history despite talk of a global recession. You need to be flexible and creative to appeal to a market that is very price and media sensitive. This does not mean you have to discount, you just need to offer a benefit to your customers through your product or service that is unique or far better than your competition. The rules have not changed, they have just become more focused.

2
TAKING THE FIRST STEPS

Hundreds and thousands of people in the UK set up their own businesses every year and their dream generally is that it will also be the passport to a more financially rewarding future and a better lifestyle. There is no right or wrong type of person to run a business, but it is worthwhile to analyse your personality and ask yourself if you are the sort of person to start a business venture. If you have motivation, commitment, determination and enthusiasm, then you have the ingredients for success, but must also be prepared to make sacrifices, work long hours, take sole responsibility and handle pressure. In addition, you will have to do things which you may find difficult, impossible or boring. Do seek out free sources of advice and talk to an adviser about your financial security and pension provisions beforehand.

You also have to think carefully about how it will affect your home life. You will need support from your family, so try to involve them right from the beginning and keep them up to date on how things are progressing. You can also use them as a sounding board and to provide feedback. You may also wish to get a good mentor on board as two heads are always better than one.

Appraise your strengths and weaknesses honestly. Make sure you have the specific skills your deli business will require. You might want to look at training or hiring an experienced staff member here, but most of all identify specifically what you do well and what you do badly.

The Small Business Advice Service (SBAS) suggests the following self-analysis:

☐ I am realistic about my capabilities.

☐ I am self-disciplined and I do not let things drift.

☐ I have the full support of my family.

☐ I am ready to put in seven days a week, if necessary.

☐ I can get on well with people.

☐ I can make careful decisions.

☐ I can cope under stress.

☐ I do not give up when the going gets tough.

☐ I can learn from mistakes.

☐ I can take advice.

☐ I am patient, and I expect a long haul.

☐ I can motivate people.

☐ I am in good health.

☐ I am enthusiastic.

☐ I know about the risks.

☐ I have specific aims.

In addition, you can decide whether you have what it takes to start your new business by using a Business Link workshop. These sessions look at the day-to-day realities of starting a business and will outline the skills and qualities you will need. The full workshop experience will go a long way in helping you answer the following questions:

☐ What do you want out of your business?

☐ Are you ready?

☐ What makes up a business plan?

☐ What is your personal survival budget?

At the end of the three-hour session you should be able to decide if starting a deli is right for you, understand what is involved and know how to access both local and national support.

Says Angus Ferguson of Demijohn deli in Edinburgh and Glasgow: 'The main issues I thought about before starting out were: Will my venture make money? Have I got the time to make it make money? Do I really want to do this? Could anyone else do this with me?'

Champion your business at all times, believe in yourself, be patient, persistent and resourceful. In the long run, the personal rewards can be extremely rewarding – so hang in there.

Developing a business sense

Apart from formal food training (see pp 10–11), you should consider a course in business skills, such as basic bookkeeping, marketing and Information Technology (IT). There are many such courses available but the following are offered by the main providers.

City & Guilds run a range of business and retail courses to help you master or improve your skills:

☐ The National Vocational Qualification (NVQ) in Business and Administration is available at different levels and covers all the key areas involved in business administration.

☐ The IT Users' Certificate features the following units to choose from: word processing, spreadsheets, databases, using the internet, email, desktop publishing, website design, relational databases, and computerised accounts.

☐ The NVQ in Customer Service prepares you for delivering good customer service.

☐ The Certificate in Bookkeeping and Accounts covers all bookkeeping techniques, while the Certificate in Computerised Accounts covers the use of the software that produces accurate, professional and well-presented accounts.

☐ The Certificate in Retailing covers everything from products and pricing to payments and security.

To find your nearest centre, contact City & Guilds at www.cityandguilds.com

ICS has a home-study Starting Your Own Business diploma course. It involves 120 hours of study and includes the following topics:

☐ You and Your Business.

☐ Setting Up Your Business.

☐ Marketing Your Business.

☐ Being an Employer.

☐ Places and Equipment.

☐ The Online Business.

☐ Planning Your Business.

ICS also runs a BTEC Level 3 Retail Management course and a BTEC Level 2 Principles of Retail course. However, for the Retail Management course you do need to hold either a GCSE equivalent to four passes at Grade C or above, or an intermediate GNVQ in an appropriate vocational area, or a BTEC First Qualification in Retail. For the Retail Management course you need to be educated to at least GCSE Standard D-G, or hold an NVQ Level 1, or alternatively a CNVQ foundation certificate.

Other courses of interest may be the Bookkeeping & Accounts and Sage Instant Accounts. For more information and costs on all courses contact ICS at www.icslearn.co.uk

Learndirect also runs a number of Business and Management courses. They are grouped together in broad categories and include:

☐ Business and the Environment.

☐ Customer Care.

☐ Customer Service NVQ.

☐ Finance and Cash Flow.

☐ Health and Care NVQ.

☐ IT for Business.

☐ Marketing.

☐ Retail Skills NVQ.

☐ Starting and Running a Business.

Contact learndirect at www.learndirect.co.uk

The Open University has a plethora of degree and diploma business courses managed through the OU Business School. The best thing here is to request copies of their brochures and a current prospectus to see what would best suit your needs. Contact The Open University at www.open.ac.uk/oubs

The NFEA offers national business support programmes/courses, such as the Let's Talk Business programme of seminars and New Entrepreneur Scholarships (NES). The Let's Talk Business Ideas programme consists of half-day events tailored to people in the early stages of deciding whether self-employment is for them, and these include vision setting, what can go wrong and how to research your idea, as well as where to go next.

The Let's Talk Starting in Business events are aimed at those who are almost ready to start their business (up to four months away). This full-day programme covers issues such as finance, marketing, time management, negotiating skills, networking and writing a business plan.

The NES programme aims to encourage enterprise in disadvantaged areas. It includes an induction and skills assessment; business support; ongoing support; and start-up support of £1,500 to purchase items that will be needed to start the business (which may include IT equipment, machinery, rent, stationery and office supplies). For more details of these programmes in your area, contact the NFEA at www.nfea.com

A wide range of marketing courses is available through the Chartered Institute of Marketing (www.cim.co.uk) which is a leading international body for marketing and business development.

Undertaking formal food training

No formal qualifications are required for starting a deli business. You will, however, be expected to have a degree of knowledge about food products and cooking styles and an interest in food trends. An NVQ in retail and a course in food hygiene should help to give you confidence in helping customers and dealing with food.

The Institute of Grocery Distribution (IGD) offers a Postgraduate Certificate in Food and Grocery Management. There are six course units, including an in-depth view of the food and grocery industry, marketing, business accounting and costing, store location, layout and merchandising. A degree or the equivalent, or at least three years' managerial experience, are the entry criteria.

If you decide to prepare food to order on site, you must hold a basic food hygiene certificate. The Royal Institute of Public Health (RIPH) at www.riph.org.uk has a set of food safety qualifications which cover the national occupational standards, including Hazard Analysis Critical Control Point (HACCP) principles.

Level 2 focuses on the importance of hygiene, the food handler's legal responsibilities and their role in monitoring food safety procedures, and how to handle, prepare and process food safely.

Level 3 includes compliance with food safety regulations, implementation of food safety management procedures, controlling hazards and supervising good practice in the workplace. For full details of course duration, content and assessment methods and to find your nearest RIPH-approved training provider, go to www.riph.org.uk

The Guild of Fine Food (www.finefoodworld.co.uk) offers one-day training seminars on cheeses, through the UK Cheese Guild, and on hams and charcuterie, through the Charcuterie Guild. Both these seminars will help you learn more about each product, improve quality, reduce stock wastage and increase sales.

Food programmes and magazines such as the BBC's *Good Food* (www.bbcgoodfood.com) or The Guild of Fine Food's retailer-targeted *Fine Food Digest* (www.finefoodworld.co.uk) can also help you stay up to date. Cultural trends may well affect the type of products you stock and the range of prepared food you supply, so it pays to be in touch with the latest developments and to add to your expertise whenever possible.

Says Fi Buchanan, of Heart Buchanan Fine Foods & Wine in Glasgow:

Self educate yourself to a high level in food, recognise your weaknesses and, if you need to, employ someone to fill the knowledge gaps. An MSC in Hospitality Management might have helped me write a business plan but I'm not a natural administrator and I need help with that side of things.

Meeting the public

Successful businesses focus on their customers. You must be a people person and able to talk to the people who come into your shop. Some may just be browsing and will walk out without buying anything, but letting them know you will go that extra mile to help them source products will help incline them to favour you with their future custom.

Think about where your customers are. Your deli will rely on local trade so it's important to know how many niche market customers you can attract to your shop. You will also have to compete against all the other food outlets in your area and rivals offering similar products. By setting yourself apart from the crowd, offering something different or special and having a pleasing disposition you will go a long way in convincing customers to buy their goods from you.

Researching your market

Your aim is to gain a detailed knowledge of your market, its size and the competition – to get an understanding of your intended customer base and customers' needs and an idea about how much money you may be able to make. Consider how the sector is going to fare in the next five years and who your most lucrative customers could be.

Quantitative research produces numerical data which can be used to determine the size of your market, how much it is worth, where the specific growth areas lie, and trends in the food industry. It can also provide details of potential customers, their likely age, gender, marital status, occupation, income, lifestyle and location. In addition, qualitative research can help you understand their attitudes and beliefs.

To be successful you need to stand out from the crowd, especially when entering the highly competitive food market. A unique selling proposition (USP) can provide a clear reason why customers will want to buy from you rather than someone else.

Try to define and consider the following:

☐ Who may wish to buy your products.

☐ What their age, sex, income and occupation may be.

☐ Whether there are any changes taking place and how these might affect what you will sell.

☐ How well your products and service must sell.

☐ How much demand there is for what you hope to sell.

☐ Who will not wish to buy what you hope to sell.

☐ What prices people would be prepared to pay.

☐ Who your competition is.

☐ How reliable your suppliers may be.

True marketing research also encompasses:

☐ Product research.

☐ Sales research.

☐ Advertising research.

According to Wenta Business Services (www.wenta.co.uk) it is important to know what is going on locally but understanding what is happening nationally can also help. Even though you may not need a national-sized market, national trends can have a significant effect at a local level. Effective market research should provide all the clues needed to forecast the future. The key information needed is:

☐ Trends in the economy – how inflation affects spending power.

☐ Trade trends – others in the same trade will often produce accurate forecasts so take the trouble to read such articles in the press.

☐ Competitor activity – if competitors are changing their product or tactics, take note of their methods.

☐ Sales analysis – scrutinise the pattern of sales in the first year to help with the next.

☐ The weather – seasonal fluctuations will affect your deli.

There are various forms of research sources you can use. The first place to go is your local library. If you are able to get to London, the newly opened Business and Intellectual Property Centre (BIPC) at the British Library (www.bl.uk/bipc) has huge resources available for people looking to set up their own business and this service is also free.

The available information includes 7,000 printed market research reports covering every kind of market you can think of, giving details of the major players, the size of their market share, the sector's potential for growth and so on. The library staff can point you in the right direction for delicatessens and retailing. You can also book a free 30-minute advice session with a member of staff to go through in detail what you require and how to get the most out of it.

If you are unable to get to London, other libraries with good business resource centres include the Norfolk and Norwich Millennium Library, Manchester's Central Library, Scotbis at the National Library of Scotland in Edinburgh, Belfast's Central Library and Flexible Support for Business (www.flexible-support-wales.gov.uk) which has several business resource centres in Wales.

You can also do a lot of market research online – from finding out about seasonal trends and demographics to researching your competitors – by using a search engine. There are plenty of existing delis with their own websites. You can find out how they describe what they do, how they package their services and the prices they charge. The internet means that small start-up businesses have as much of a chance as bigger competitors of finding the information they need. Make sure the websites you use are reliable and contain up-to-date information.

Another good place to start is Business Link; its information service can tell you what research is available and how to get it. If you need to commission market research, then Business Link advisers can help you to draw up a brief and find a market researcher to do the work.

Other useful sources include the National Statistics Office (www.statistics.gov.uk) BERR (www.berr.gov.uk) and the Chamber of Commerce in your area. Two useful market research sites are www.freshminds.co.uk and www.snapdata.co.uk. You can find information on market trends from Mintel (www.mintel.co.uk), Key Note (www.keynote.co.uk), Euromonitor (www.euromonitor.co.uk) and Datamonitor (www.datamonitor.co.uk).

UpMyStreet (www.upmystreet.com) provides postcode local statistics and socio-economic profiles for local areas. In addition, if you join The Guild of Fine Food you will be able to access the data which has been collected from their members which may be extremely useful.

THE MARKETING MIX

Once you have completed your research and looked at every angle of your business, you can start to pull all the information together to enable you to generate a plan of action. The success of a good marketing plan boils down to balancing a good mix of marketing solutions.

The marketing mix examines your product to help you decide whether it is in demand or in decline; looks at the price you intend to charge and the best type of pricing policy to exploit the need; investigates the best location; and homes in on the best type of promotion you should use for the best results.

You will need to take a long, hard look at the competition in your area and identify how many other outlets are selling delicatessen lines. It may be that you will only be competing directly against a few of these outlets because you plan to set up a very specialist type of store, maybe by stocking only Mediterranean or local product ranges.

By visiting all the competing shops in your area, you can establish how helpful and knowledgeable the staff are, their opening hours, how the products are displayed, whether the premises and fittings are modern or more traditional, the range of products stocked, prices charged, and the kinds of customers they attract.

This should indicate if there is a gap in the market for a delicatessen specialising in a certain type of product. For example, none of the delicatessens in your area might offer Italian cheese or olive oil, or Spanish hams, sherry and vinegar.

Further research your area by using the Yellow Pages (www.yell.com) and Thomson Local (www.thomsonlocal.com). Many supermarkets and department stores now also have their own delicatessen counters which will be in direct competition. Consumers may use these outlets during their weekly shop or because of their long opening hours, convenience and parking availability.

There is also a range of online food retailers who specialise in attracting those customers who wish to buy specialised foods and ingredients via the internet. Other competitors will include mail order gourmet food retailers. If you look at www.britishmailorder.com you will find a directory of businesses providing high-quality food via the mail. Small independent ethnic food retailers also attract customers looking for specific and authentic foods. Kabayan Oriental Foods (www.kabayanorientalfoods.co.uk) has a directory of suppliers, producers and retailers of speciality, ethnic and gourmet foodstuffs.

Farmers' markets and farm shops often sell similar goods to those available in delicatessens, including smoked meats, cordials, pickles and preserves. The Directory of Farmers' Markets (www.farmersmarkets.net) and the Farm Retail Association (www.farmshopping.net) have information about markets and shops across the UK.

There is also www.scottishfarmersmarkets.co.uk and www.fmiw.co.uk (for Northern Ireland go to http://thefoody.com/regions/irelandfm.html). It's a good idea to visit these outlets in your area. Check the listing of regional food groups in Chapter 7 Planning for success.

Competition is a very healthy thing, but you need to do constant research as a result. Never ever be complacent.

Identifying potential customers

Your customers will mainly be members of the public who have an appreciation of good food and wine. These may be targeted by a certain range of foodstuffs, for example Polish, or those looking for an alternative to mass-produced convenience foods. There are also those consumers who are more environmentally conscious and aware of food miles who are specifically interested in regionally and locally produced food. Some customers may have particular dietary requirements, such as vegetarian, vegan, gluten-free, wheat-free and non-dairy.

According to the British Retail Consortium (BRC), www.brc.co.uk, baby boomer consumers have more money at their disposal than any other age group. Those aged between 35 and 54 will generally earn larger salaries and will have accumulated more wealth than those who are younger than them. They are also more likely to be in employment, unlike many older customers who may rely on their pensions alone.

However, there are significant variations in wealth and the amount of disposable income available in this age group. Some people will still have young families and must support them financially, whereas others will have seen their children move out of the family home and can now spend more of their income on themselves. Youth consumers, aged between 15 and 24, spend proportionally far less on food and groceries than the general population.

3
DEALING WITH MONEY MATTERS

If you are setting up a business, finding finance can be a struggle, but without sufficient funding your business will fail. You need to have a sound business to attract money, but you need money to build a sound business. Without a track record, finding funding is difficult. There is an old saying that there is never a shortage of people offering you money when you don't need it – what bankers term lending you a brolly when it's not going to rain.

The Confederation of Business Industry (CBI) says that sufficient access to finance in the UK is crucial. 'Affordable and appropriate finance enables businesses to operate efficiently and grow. It facilitates business start-ups and enables them to expand operations to meet demand.' The CBI has called for the £250,000 to £3 million equity gap facing small- and medium-sized businesses (SMEs) to be addressed and has voiced the need for more mezzanine finance schemes.

This aside, there are numerous sources of funding but each one has advantages and disadvantages peculiar to it.

Raising finance

To begin with, look at your own personal savings and assets. If you have a maturing ISA, an inheritance, a redundancy payment, a life insurance policy, or can take out a second mortgage, you might actually have the 'wealth' to fund your business yourself. Cash in the bank can be a useful source of working capital to help you during the first few months.

However, only consider securing a loan against personal assets if you want to make a long-term investment in your business. You can then factor the repayment costs into your business plan. Raising the money yourself is a good way of keeping control of your business and means you don't owe money to anyone else.

Most banks and building societies offer commercial loans but will only lend you money against some form of security. The first option is to agree to an overdraft amount that your bank will let you borrow without notice. In return, you pay interest on the sum borrowed and possibly a service or set-up charge. Interest is usually calculated on a daily basis so you pay only for what you borrow.

Overdrafts are useful for temporary financing or fluctuating cash shortages, such as seasonal fluctuations or having to pay suppliers before you receive payment from customers. They are quick and convenient to arrange as well as flexible. Your overdraft should only be used temporarily to pay for day-to-day business running costs, such as paying bills and wages or buying stock.

If you can persuade the bank that you will be able to generate a steady and predictable cash flow, you may be able to take out a small, unsecured loan. However, a long-term loan may be the best way to finance your business. Many run for a fixed period of one to ten years. Loan repayments must be made monthly and will include bank finance costs. For any borrowing you will need to provide security, either a personal guarantee (assets) or a guarantee from a third party who will be liable to pay the debt if you default.

Credit and charge cards are a variable and convenient short-term means of borrowing cash, paying bills and making purchases, regardless of how much is in your bank account. Using these cards can reduce your bank charges because you are writing fewer cheques. They are also an expeditious and convenient method of payment and can give you up to 56 days of free credit. The itemised billing means that you can analyse your spending patterns quickly and clearly, which helps with your bookkeeping.

At the moment, there is huge competition in the credit card market with many companies currently offering 0% interest on balance transfers for 12 months. You could take advantage of this by continually transferring your balance from one company to another, effectively borrowing for nothing. Look out for the annual fixed charge and remember that if you don't clear your monthly balance within the specified time, you will incur stiff charges. Credit cards should only be used as a short-term funding solution and you may find that a bank loan is a more suitable option if the borrowing is ongoing.

While about two-thirds of all businesses go to their bank for funding, there are three other common sources of money that could help start up your business: family and friends; specialist backers; and grants.

Family and friends

You could ask friends and family. If you do, go for either a loan or an investment. If it is a loan you should agree a fixed repayment period and rate of interest. However, they may be willing to offer a low interest loan, or one with no interest attached at all. If they make an investment they will hold equity in your company in the form of profits. They will expect a percentage of the profits and the ability to sell their stake in the business at some time in the future.

It is important that any loan or investment should be underpinned with a formally drawn-up agreement explaining everyone's liabilities, obligations and expectations in order to avoid damaging relationships in the future.

Specialist backers

According to The Capital Fund (www.thecapitalfund.co.uk) the market for finance which is aimed at young, growing businesses in the UK has come a long way in the past 25 years. Venture capitalists (VCs) are professional fund management companies prepared to give potential high-fliers significant backing.

They tend to have high minimum investment levels and are not usually interested in the level of funding that small companies will need. VCs invest money, rather than lend it, in return for shares in the business and normally look for a minimum return of between 30% and 40% a year over five years.

The process of raising venture capital will take about three to six months and they typically only invest in 2% to 5% of the proposals put before them. Check with the British Venture Capital Association (www.bvca.co.uk) for some of the UK's principal institutions.

Business angels

A business angel is an informal venture capitalist who is willing to provide equity finance to a small business. They are private individuals, normally entrepreneurs or retired executives, who will expect to receive shares in your business in return for providing the cash to start up your venture. They may also be prepared to share their experience, advice and contacts to help your business really take off.

Typically, a business angel would be prepared to invest between £10,000 and £750,000. The Chamber of Commerce states that business angels are a significant source of start-up and early-stage capital for companies without a proven track record. A business plan based on powerful market research is essential when contacting these organisations.

Potential sources of business angels may include your bank, your local Business Link, or one of the organisations that exist to bring the two together. You can also find one through the British Business Angels Association (BBAA) at www.bbaa.org.uk. Look through the online member directory and choose a business angel most suited to your needs, in terms of specialisation, investment criteria and geographic location.

The business sections of a number of newspapers will also include advertisements from investors and from businesses looking for finance.

Grants

If you have no security to offer, you may be entitled to some form of a grant. There are a number of grants available to small businesses from central and local government and a range of organisations and trusts (see 'Seeking government help and support', pp. 39–40).

However, many sources will require you to raise half of the amount you need.

Remember that all lenders and investors look for a good business plan, strong financial controls, personal commitment and a well-researched opportunity. Don't be daunted – they need you as much as you need them.

Information needed

Before approaching anyone for finance, you will need to prepare the following information:

- ☐ Cash flow forecast – how much cash will be available in the business and how you will monitor this cash flow.

- ☐ Balance sheet forecast – showing fixed assets (equipment) and current assets (stock and debtors), how your assets are financed and the expected net worth of the business.

- ☐ Business plan – (see 'Writing a business plan', pp. 22–24).

- ☐ Personal budgets – work out your personal expenditure (mortgage payments, electricity, gas and phone bills) as this will show how much money you need to take out of the business.

- ☐ Forms of identification – any investor will want proof of your identity.

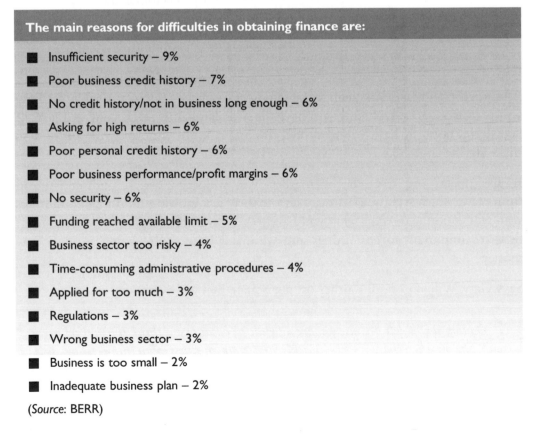

The main reasons for difficulties in obtaining finance are:

- ■ Insufficient security – 9%
- ■ Poor business credit history – 7%
- ■ No credit history/not in business long enough – 6%
- ■ Asking for high returns – 6%
- ■ Poor personal credit history – 6%
- ■ Poor business performance/profit margins – 6%
- ■ No security – 6%
- ■ Funding reached available limit – 5%
- ■ Business sector too risky – 4%
- ■ Time-consuming administrative procedures – 4%
- ■ Applied for too much – 3%
- ■ Regulations – 3%
- ■ Wrong business sector – 3%
- ■ Business is too small – 2%
- ■ Inadequate business plan – 2%

(*Source*: BERR)

Writing a business plan

Anyone planning to set up in business should have a plan. Trying to run your business without planning is like floating aimlessly at sea in a fog. You need to build an operational short-, medium-, and long-term plan and then continually measure your progress against it. As you gather more experience and data, you can change and improve this plan.

A business plan is not only necessary for raising finance it also has a role to play in everyday business management and at critical moments in the life of your business. When you are faced with customer demands, tax deadlines, VAT returns and many other 'business as usual' problems, it can seem hard to justify devoting any time at all to drawing up a business plan.

According to Wenta Business Services (www.wenta.co.uk) the reasons for compiling a business plan include:

- ☐ To get your ideas clear in your own mind.

- ☐ To have this act as a discussion document with professional advisers.

- ☐ To use this as an application to obtain finance.

- ☐ To minimise your risk of failure.

A business plan makes you analyse the resources you have – finance, people, facilities and premises – to see whether you have the wherewithal to reach your end goal. If you don't, not only have you identified this as a risk but you can work out how to make up the shortfall.

It also makes you research the markets you will compete in both today and tomorrow, which will then help you ensure there is a growing number of customers who will continue to want what you have to sell. Even if you plan to work alone at first, it's important to cost things and work out how you're going to make any money.

Says Gary Williamson, of Corner on the Square deli in Inverness:

Do not start a deli because you are a foodie or because you think the market needs you. The market changes very quickly and your business plan must follow suit. Running a deli is a daily commitment to hard work and without the continued support of finance, staff and customers it simply will not work.

Your plan

This should include:

- **An executive summary** This highlights the most important points of your business plan and if finance is required, the amount should be stated here. This should appear at the front of your document and acts as the introduction.

- **Nature of the business** This explains clearly and concisely the nature of your business and your potential market. Include an outline of your business proposal and a strengths, weaknesses, opportunities and threats (SWOT) analysis. Strengths and weaknesses are internal characteristics of your business; opportunities and threats are external.

- **Owner/manager/key personnel** This briefly sets out the skills and experience of those who will manage your business.

- **Objectives** This explains the broad aims of your business and your short-term (first year), medium-term (the next one to three years), and long-term (five-year span) objectives.

- **Market research** This outlines the key characteristics of buyers in your target segments, such as their age, gender, location and income. You must also list your competitors and their strengths and weaknesses.

- **Marketing plan** This is an outline of how you will market and promote your deli.

- **Premises, fittings and vehicles** This gives details of the proposed premises, size, location, tenure, cost, and next rent review.

- **Financial projections** These will include the profit and cashflow forecast on a month-by-month basis for the first 12 months. Show how much finance the business might need. Detail how much, when and in which form you will need it. State what the finance will be used for and include an estimate of your personal wealth and survival income.

Remember, many business plans are too long. Keep yours concise, yet comprehensive and well-considered (about 12 pages) in all. Put a cover on your document and give it a title and a contents page. Make sure it looks professional and is also accurate and realistic.

Business Link, the Small Business Advice Service (SBAS), and most banks have a business plan template online where all the core elements are clearly set out for you.

The sample plan on the SBAS website (www.smallbusinessadvice.org.uk) allows you to fill in the sections and submit the plan to an online adviser for comments. The service will identify an Accredited Business Adviser in your locality who will contact you by email within a day or so and invite you to submit your plan for review.

At the Alliance & Leicester Commercial Bank (www.alliance-leicester commercialbank.co.uk) you can download the free Business Planner software. It gives you interactive templates, a cash flow forecast, a profit and loss forecast, and contains helpful guidance notes right the way through. Alternatively, you may feel better if you consult your own business adviser or accountant.

Top ten tips for writing a business plan:

- Write from your audience's perspective.
- Include enough detail to ensure the reader has sufficient information to make an informed decision.
- Research your market thoroughly.
- Understand the competition.
- Clearly describe the investment opportunity.
- Ensure all the key areas are covered in the plan.
- Document the costs in full and predict your sales realistically.
- Include an executive summary.
- Have your plan independently reviewed.
- Detail its implementation.

Deciding on the location

Finding the right premises for your deli is one of the biggest decisions you'll have to make. It will involve a number of factors, including the geographical location, its affordability and the facilities available. Ideally there should be plenty of passing trade, some parking nearby, and room for delivery vehicles.

Being in a specialised niche market may mean you are unable to justify a site on the high street. Perhaps you should instead look for an area with a concentration of office workers who might be key customers. And don't under- or over-estimate the space you need, as you may end up being in the wrong premises with a lengthy lease.

Says Michael Cogswell, Location Services Manager of Locate East Sussex:

> ❝ *Like any business the deli owner needs to be clear who their customers will be, which should be included in the business plan, and should target their 'offer' to those customers. I would contend that a part of that offer will be to locate the business in a town, or part of a town, where those customers are likely to shop and in premises which are likely to appeal to the customer.'* ❞

If you intend to lease or buy, check out the location thoroughly. Look at the number and kind of shoppers, the facilities, and the local crime rate. A town location means you could attract more passing trade and create a better image. However, rent and rates will be higher. Maintenance, insurance and electricity costs should also be within your budget.

Says Fi Buchanan, of Heart Buchanan Fine Food & Wine in Glasgow:

> ❝ *It takes about a year to find the right place and then you need to monitor how many people walk past. It's almost impossible to buy a property as people are buying up shops to rent – it's a good pension plan for them.* ❞

Personal contacts may know of suitable premises, or could suggest other people to consult. Premises are also advertised online, in local newspapers and property magazines. *Daltons Weekly* (www.daltons.co.uk) covers property across the whole country. Business Link, commercial property agents, or your local council will also be able to advise you accordingly.

Many economic development organisations, such as Locate East Sussex, run websites which will include a vacant property database to which commercial property agents contribute. A trawl through the websites of commercial property agents operating in the area should also yield results.

Says Michael Cogswell:

> ❝ *An informal discussion with an established commercial property agent and/or Town Centre Manager, who are often employed by local authorities and are operating in the chosen area, should also provide an opportunity to acquire vital market intelligence for the business plan, such as how much rent to pay, how often properties of the kind required come on to the market, what is the trading history of the town, and how previous deli operations have fared. TCMs are often ex-retailers with a wealth of knowledge and contacts to call on.* ❞

If you use a commercial property agency, give them a detailed spec. Decide on the size you will need, any special needs, your maximum price (including VAT) and any annual charges. Property size is usually calculated on a square footage rate, so work out how much space you will need and base your search on that.

Angus Ferguson, Managing Director of Demijohn deli in Ednburgh and Glasgow, says you need to be patient:

Never take the first offer and always negotiate for a lower price. Ask other shopkeepers in the area as they will give you very sound advice on trading conditions and price.

Once you have found the right place, you may need to carry out a survey of the structural state of the building. The Royal Institute of Chartered Surveyors will advise you on surveyors in your area. When renting, you will normally be expected to pay your landlord's solicitor's and surveyor's fees.

Also check the property grading and see if you will be able to do renovations, if there is any history of subsidence or damp, and whether there has been any flooding in the area. Ask your solicitor to request a flood report from an environmental company which provides information about flood areas, such as Groundsure, Landmark or Homecheck.

Make sure you are on the right side of complicated regulations, such as environment health rules. As a food business, you must register the premises at least 28 days before you plan to open. The building will also have to meet disability discrimination laws and health and safety regulations.

Have a look at all the hidden costs, such as security, rates and service charges, insurance premiums, and your local council's business rates. Lawyers for Business (www.lawsociety.org.uk/choosingandusing/helpyourbusiness/foryourbusiness.law) provides 30 minutes of free legal advice on premises and leases.

Says Gary Williamson, of Corner on the Square deli in Inverness:

Location is crucial. We were lucky in that we found the premises almost before the business idea fully materialised. We struck a deal with the landlord to sell to us at the end of a five-year lease. The gamble paid off for us.

Buying v leasing

A commercial property is usually occupied on a freehold or leasehold basis. With freehold you can use the building as you wish, but if you have a limited business financial history or none at all you may find it difficult to obtain a commercial mortgage and be obliged to cough up a substantial deposit. Commercial mortgages run for between five and 25 years, the length of which usually determines the interest rate you will pay.

Most lenders will expect to receive 20% to 30% of the asking price as a down-payment. Therefore, freehold carries a big financial risk for start-ups; you'll need to generate enough profit to keep up the repayments and cover any increases in interest rates. On the other hand, leasing doesn't require a huge capital outlay at the start, there is less financial risk, the lease is usually renewable and you will have the right to stay. The down side here is that you'll have restricted use of the property, including the right to make alterations, and the terms of the lease can be complicated. Check the small print of your lease agreement and look out for:

- The length of the lease and who owns it.

- Break clauses.

- Who has responsibility for repairs and renewals.

- How often the rent is reviewed.

- Any service charges.

Negotiate your contract and see if you can get a break clause if you need to vacate earlier than planned. In addition, paying a solicitor to examine a contract is often money well spent.

Says Michael Cogswell of Locate East Sussex:

The decision whether to buy premises relates to the financial position of the business and the level of operating and financial risk that the proprietor is prepared to be exposed to. Renting premises, which may be the only way forward at an early stage in the business lifecycle, exposes businesses to less financial risk, depending on the length of lease taken – the shorter it is the less risk there is, but it may increase the operating risk as the deli proprietor is then in the hands of his landlord with potentially more instability.

The decision to buy might leave the proprietor in a difficult position if things go wrong, although he has an asset which could be leased on to other businesses; it might be seen as a blessing if the business succeeds. Other factors, such as a flat above the shop, if included in the purchase might make the decision to buy less of a business and more of a lifestyle decision.

Securing your shop

Assess the safety and security of your premises. You will need effective locks and secure windows, while smoke detectors and a burglar alarm are necessities. Think about how you will protect your equipment and business data. You will need to back up your computer data regularly.

Understanding the legal requirements

There is a wide range of laws to protect businesses, the general public and employees. You should, therefore, have a basic understanding of the law and how it affects you and your business. Your solicitor will be able to tell you about existing trading laws, such as the Consumer Protection Act and the Sale and Supply of Goods Act (see Chapter 5 and Chapter 9 for more information).

The following is meant as a guidance only on how to trade and name your business. You should seek professional advice before making any business decisions that may have legal consequences.

Structuring your business

When you set your company up, you need to decide at an early stage how you intend to structure it as your status can have both legal and practical implications. There are four main business structures:

- ☐ Sole trader (self-employed).

- ☐ Partnership (self-employed people working together).

- ☐ Limited company.

- ☐ Co-operative.

SOLE TRADER

Most people who first set out in business will do so as sole traders. This simply means you have complete control and are solely responsible for your business's profit and loss. Sole trader is the simplest, quickest, and cheapest form of business to set up and has its own advantages and disadvantages which need to be considered before you begin.

If you choose to be a sole trader you will be self-employed and personally liable for any debts the business incurs. On the upside, you get to keep all the profits you make. Start-up formalities are also minimal and the costs are low.

Sole traders can employ other people. They are able to give a more personal service to customers. As such you are also able to make changes within your business very quickly. However, there is an unlimited liability for debts. So, if your business loses money you may wind up having to sell your personal assets.

You need to keep simple accounts and complete a self-assessment tax return to HM Revenue & Customs (HMRC) at www.hmrc.gov.uk each year, detailing your income and expenses. You must also maintain records showing all your income and expenses. To become a sole trader, you must register as self-employed with HMRC within the first three months of starting up. If you fail to do so you will face a penalty of £100.

Tax and National Insurance (NI) payments are likely to be lower than for a limited company structure, but sole traders are personally liable for their business debts and they are also entitled to fewer social security benefits. You must pay income tax on any profits your business makes in the form of National Insurance Contributions (NICs), which will be either Class 2 or Class 4. HMRC offers local one-day courses on how to become a sole trader.

In addition, you need to register for VAT if your turnover is going to be more than £60,000 a year.

PARTNERSHIP

A partnership is a business arrangement where two or more people (up to a maximum of 20) are self-employed and in business together to make a profit. This way all the partners share the business costs, profits and debts. Partnerships work well when each partner brings a different skill or area of expertise to the business and the workload is divided up to reflect each of the partners' strengths. You will then need to consider if an ordinary or limited partnership would be best for your business. In an ordinary partnership the partner or partners would take on unlimited liability for any debts incurred by the business and all profits would be shared equally.

Limited partnerships accept a limited liability to the amount invested and, while the profits are shared equally, full responsibility and control of the business remain with the ordinary partners. Limited partners are often seen as 'sleeping partners' as they do not directly involve themselves with the company they have invested in. While there are no legal obligations for ordinary partners, it is recommended that a partnership agreement be arranged to legalise the partnership, as this will help to avoid any disputes which may arise.

It is also recommended that a solicitor should be brought in to collate this agreement and that they would include the following points:

☐ The amount of capital each partner will invest.

☐ The profit ratio dependent on the amount invested.

☐ The debt liabilities – whether for an ordinary or limited partnership.

Should it be decided that a partnership would prove the best way forward for your business, you would first need to decide how many partners could benefit the business. Then consider how you would like the partners to integrate within the company. Finally, try to estimate the following:

☐ The partners or their liabilities to drive the business forward.

☐ Their leadership qualities and management experience.

☐ Their level of specialist knowledge and expertise.

☐ The level of trust you would associate with the partners.

☐ Their seniority and control over the business.

☐ The rules for admitting new partners.

☐ The rules for ending the partnership.

A LIMITED COMPANY

Setting up a limited company is the most common alternative. Even though you will own it and work for it, a limited company is a separate entity, which means you will only be personally liable for any debts in exceptional circumstances. Compared to sole tradership, there will be more administration required by you and NI payments may be higher.

If you decide to start a limited company, most people doing so will use a registration or formation agent, solicitor or accountant. A limited company must be registered with Companies House. Formation agents, such as the National Business Register, use their own software which works directly with the Companies House system. Typically costs start at about £200, depending on the level of service you require.

A key advantage to using an agent is the advice they can give you on compiling the necessary documents and implementing the correct structure for your business. Companies House does not offer this service when registering. Alternatively, you can use an online registration company which usually costs about £80 to £100 including fees, but this can take three to eight days.

A LIMITED LIABILITY COMPANY

A Limited Liability Company (LLC) is one where the shareholders have limited liability for the company's debts. Their liability is restricted to the value of the shares that they own or the guarantees that they sign up to. A Limited Liability Partnership (LLP) aims to combine the flexibility of a partnership arrangement with the benefits of limited liability. It is doubtful you will choose either of these legal structures in a delicatessen set up.

COMMUNITY INTEREST COMPANY AND CO-OPS

A Community Interest Company (CIC) is a new type of company. Essentially they are limited companies who want to use their profits and assets for the public good. CIC's are designed for social enterprises, including local community enterprises, social firms and mutual organisations, such as co-operatives. Co-operatives are businesses which are collectively owned and controlled by the people who work in it. At least two people must be involved. For more information contact the Community Interest Companies Regulator at www.cicregulator.gov.uk.

Naming your business

Another important part of the planning stage is to choose a catchy name for your business. This should portray a certain image and provide good marketing potential. While you are no longer required to register your business name with any government department, there are laws about using certain names and disclosing certain details of ownership.

If you are a sole trader, you can trade under your own name, or choose a different business name. A partnership can trade under the names of all the partners or a business name. A limited company or limited liability partnership can trade under its registered name or use a different business name. If you buy an off-the-shelf company you can apply to change the registered name.

To further protect your business name from use by others you can register it as a trade mark, or a domain name, or both. The Patent Office regulates trade mark registration. An agent can check for names already registered as trade marks. This usually costs from £50 to £80. To check web domain names free of charge, search at a name registration service such as www.netnames.co.uk.

When you have decided on the name, you must check that there is no other business already trading under that name. You can do this through Companies House (www.companieshouse.gov.uk) or by using a company registration agent.

If you do not trade under your exact name on stationery, shop signs, or bank details, you need to let your customers know your name and the business address where you can be contacted. For example, if your name is 'S. Smith' and your business trades as 'S. Smith', you do not have to disclose these. However, if your business stationery and banking details are 'S. Smith's Deli', you have to disclose.

Certain names are not allowed and they must also not be misleading or likely to cause confusion with an existing business. Names judged to be offensive are also banned by Companies House. Certain words are prohibited by law, for example British, Royal and Bank. The Companies House booklet GBF2 details prohibited words.

Approaching business banks

Almost every report you read says that starting a business can be a complicated and daunting experience. However, this does not have to be the case if you have your finances in place and have established support from your bank. There are many banks and lots of offers to choose from, but the following operate on a national level:

Alliance & Leicester Commercial Bank, www.alliance-leicester.co.uk
Bank of Scotland, www.bankofscotland.co.uk
Barclays Bank, www.barclays.co.uk
Clydesdale Bank, www.cbonline.co.uk
HSBC Bank, www.ukbusiness.hsbc.com
Lloyds TSB Bank, www.lloydstsb.co.uk
NatWest, www.natwest.com
The Co-operative Bank, www.co-operativebank.co.uk
The Royal Bank of Scotland, www.rbs.co.uk
Triodos Bank, www.triodos.co.uk
Bank of Ireland, www.bankofireland.co.uk
First Trust Bank, www.firsttrustbank.co.uk
Northern Bank, www.northernbank.co.uk
Ulster Bank, www.ulsterbank.co.uk

According to the FSB, access to a reliable banking infrastructure is crucial for small businesses. It says:

> *There needs to be more competition in the banking sector, as more than 70% of small businesses continue to use the four main banks to provide their banking needs. Switching between banks is still causing problems and small businesses often do not have the resources, especially in terms of time, that it requires to switch business accounts.*

It is also important to have a named contact with a working knowledge of your business at your local branch and to be able to access your branch at your convenience. Cautions FSB:

> *The move towards a greater use of call centres has been highly detrimental to customer services and banks should take steps to improve their services to help serve the needs of the 99% of all businesses in the UK who are small businesses.*

WORKING WITH YOUR BANK

There is no harm in getting in touch with a few different banks and talking through what you need. The key to getting the best out of your bank is to establish a good relationship with your main contact, whether they are the local manager or the bank's Small Business Adviser. The more they understand about you and your business, the more they can help you. To consolidate relationships, keep your manager up to date with your performance, new plans, and with any changes in your business.

In addition to this relationship, find a bank that offers the most favourable terms, including any charges for paying in and withdrawing money, as well as interest rates on overdrafts and credit balances. Find out about their full range of services and their online business banking facilities.

Compare a minimum of three accounts using a financial information provider such as Moneyfacts (www.moneyfacts.co.uk). All banks will offer a plethora of literature on their small business accounts which you can pick up at a branch or check on individual websites.

A number of banks offer free banking for set periods for new businesses. However, do look beyond these deals and find out how much you will end up paying to maintain your account. Although the major banks have improved their interest rates on business current accounts at the request of the government, these do vary widely.

You may well decide to keep your personal account and business account at different banks. If you are a sole trader you could use your personal account, but other business structures will require you to set up a separate business account. More than likely, you will accept payment from customers by credit or debit card and, therefore, you will need to open a merchant account. There are monthly card charges payable to your merchant account provider.

A selection of popular accounts
Abbey (www.anbusiness.com)
- ☐ Free day-to-day banking.
- ☐ Interest on transferred accounts.
- ☐ No maximum/minimum turnover.
- ☐ No monthly standing charge.
- ☐ Interest paid on credit balances.
- ☐ An authorised overdraft at 5.9% ABR.
- ☐ Telephone/online banking.
- ☐ Free credits and debits.
- ☐ A cheque charge of 50p, 100 cheque deposits a month free forever.
- ☐ Free direct debit/standing orders forever.

To benefit permanently from free day-to-day banking you will need to keep your bank account in credit and operate within specified transaction limits. Banks will offer a local Business Relationship Manager for help with finance solutions.

Alliance & Leicester Commercial Bank
- ☐ Two years' business banking completely free.
- ☐ No minimum balance of funding requirements.
- ☐ No standard transaction charges.
- ☐ Interest paid if in credit.
- ☐ Authorised overdraft rate negotiable.
- ☐ Free internet business guidance service.
- ☐ Free legal and tax advice.
- ☐ Bank by internet, fax, phone or at any Post Office.
- ☐ No cheque charge.
- ☐ No charge on direct debit/standing order.

It is only available through the Business Builder Current Account. Their business start-up checklist will make sure you have considered all the issues involved in starting up your business successfully. A dedicated switching service will also make sure the move from your old bank is as easy as possible.

Bank of Scotland
- Business current account.
- Assistance for start-ups for the first 12 months.
- No transaction charges.
- Interest paid if in credit.
- No overdraft fees for first 12 months.
- Telephone/online banking.
- A cheque charge of 53p.
- Direct debit/standing order charge of 34p/45p.

Introductory offers apply to individuals setting up their first business bank account within the first 12 months of trading. There is also access to a Relationship Manager.

Barclays Bank
- Business current account.
- Free banking for 12 months for start-ups.
- Flexible banking.
- Pay in/out charges.
- Telephone/online banking available.
- Cheque charge of 28p.
- No direct debits/standing order charge.

You will have access to a local Business Manager, support during and outside working hours, and free business seminars.

Co-op Bank
- Clarity account.
- No introductory offers.
- Standing charge of £15 a month.
- Interest paid if in credit.
- Authorised overdraft charge of 11.89%.
- Telephone/internet banking available.
- No cheques charge.
- No direct debit/standing order charge.

You will have a dedicated telephone-based Relationship Management Team who will advise you on all bank issues. Free advice on tax and legal issues via a helpline. Free commercial legal protection is available worth up to £50,000.

HSBC

- ☐ Business Direct account.
- ☐ Free banking for 18 months.
- ☐ No standing charges.
- ☐ Interest paid if in credit.
- ☐ Authorised overdraft is negotiable.
- ☐ Telephone/internet banking available.
- ☐ Cheque charge of £1.
- ☐ No charge for direct debit/standing order.

Lloyds TSB

- ☐ Business Extra account.
- ☐ Free day-to-day banking for 18 months.
- ☐ Standing charge of £3 a month.
- ☐ Interest paid if in credit.
- ☐ Authorised overdraft is negotiable.
- ☐ Internet electronic banking available.
- ☐ All internet banking, phonebank and phonebank express payments cost 20p each.
- ☐ Cheque charge of 60p.
- ☐ Standing order charge of 30p.

Provide free business planning tool to help get your business moving, including the free *Getting Started in Business* book. You will also have access to a named Business Manager.

NatWest

- ☐ Start Up account.
- ☐ Free 24 months' banking for businesses that have been trading for 12 months.
- ☐ Fee-free Business MasterCard or fee-free £500 overdraft for the first year.
- ☐ No standing charge.
- ☐ No credit interest but other savings products available.
- ☐ Overdraft negotiable.
- ☐ Online, telephone and mobile banking available.
- ☐ No cheques charge.
- ☐ Direct debit/standing order no charge.

Start-up customers are assigned their own local Business Manager who will be their main point of contact and will assist with all their business banking needs. The business manager can be contacted by a direct line telephone number or by email and can meet customers face to face. Business managers offer free advice and guidance.

Free business planning is also available, which includes a template to produce a professional business plan plus essential tools to help develop a business.

Royal Bank of Scotland
  ☐ Business Banking Direct.
  ☐ No standing charge.
  ☐ No interest paid if in credit.
  ☐ Overdraft negotiable.
  ☐ Telephone/internet banking available.
  ☐ No cheque charge.
  ☐ No standing order charge.

Some services are backed up by a local Business Relationship Manager.

Training
NatWest offers a start-up training course. When you subscribe to the course online you will initially receive comprehensive factsheets covering both your location and your business idea. You will then start to receive the first seven daily email newsletters aimed at the key topics facing anyone starting out in business.

Day 1: Planning and information about your business idea.
Day 2: Researching your market.
Day 3: Choosing premises.
Day 4: Finding the money to start your business.
Day 5: Starting up legally.
Day 6: Who you need to tell before you start up.
Day 7: Who to ask for help, information, finance and support in your region.

Once you have completed these daily emails you will start to receive a weekly series of more in-depth newsletters.

Week 1: Thinking ahead.
Week 2: The risks and how to minimise them.
Week 3: Protecting your ideas and business interest.
Week 4: Grants and cash to get started.
Week 5: Legal issues to consider.
Week 6: What to do before you start selling.

After you complete the course you will continue to receive a monthly newsletter containing information and guidance that will help you as you start and run your own business. You can register through the business section of www.natwest.com.

Accessing online banking

Most banks these days offer flexible banking that's online or telephone banking that gives you instant access to your business and personal bank accounts. Many banks and building societies give competitive interest rates to online customers. Business online banking services are designed to accommodate computer users with varying levels of experience. In addition, there are usually help sections and customer support contact details in case you need further assistance.

If you're too busy dealing with customers, orders, employees and the many other business-related matters that can arise during the day, you might need to deal with your accounts in the evening or at the weekend. Banking online allows you to carry out your transactions at a time that suits you. If you are using bookkeeping software you may be able to download information directly from your online bank accounts into your books. This makes it easier to reconcile your business records with your bank accounts, since actual details of your income and expenditure will be automatically entered into your books.

Online banking allows you to reduce the impact of bank charges on your business finances. Instant access to account information helps you to avoid the sorts of incidents that can lead to unnecessary bank fees, such as unauthorised overdraft fees.

One disadvantage, though, is that online banking may seem a little too impersonal if you like a face-to-face relationship with your bank. Telephone banking can also be a useful alternative for managing your business account if you don't have time to go to your bank. It is particularly suitable if you regularly transfer money between different accounts (current, deposit, business, personal) but, as with online banking, you still have to visit a branch to deposit your takings.

In the past, money transferred between banks would disappear for up to four days. In 2007, the banks made an estimated £30 million a year in interest from this delay. Now there is a banking scheme for one-day cash transfers over the telephone or on the internet. Customers can make one-off payments up to a maximum value of £10,000 over the telephone or via the internet, which will leave their account and arrive at the destination account on the same day.

The Faster Payments Service has been developed by 13 banks, which include: Abbey, Alliance & Leicester, Barclays, Citi, Clydesdale and Yorkshire Banks, Co-operative Bank, HBOS, HSBC, Lloyds TSB, Nationwide Building Society, Northern Bank, Northern Rock, NatWest, Royal Bank of Scotland, and Ulster Bank.

Seeking government help and support

In March 2008, the government launched a new Enterprise Strategy to make the UK the most enterprising economy in the world and the best place to start and grow a business. According to the Department for Business, Enterprise & Regulatory Reform (BERR), it is designed to unlock the nation's entrepreneurial talents; boost enterprise skills and knowledge; help new and existing businesses get funding to start up and grow; and ease the burden of regulation – particularly on small firms which feel its impact most.

Research has shown that businesses receiving support and advice are more likely to flourish as a result, gaining a competitive advantage and creating high value companies that benefit local communities. Most of this assistance comes from private or third sector providers. However, assistance from the government can help address market failures or equity gaps. Consequently, the government spends £2.5 billion a year in directly supporting businesses to meet the challenges they face, by providing publicly funded grants, subsidies, advice and other support services. Of this, 40% is local funding.

Some companies, particularly time- and cash-strapped small- and medium-sized businesses, are put off seeking help as a result of confusion over the numerous schemes, multiple providers and a lack of co-ordination. An annual survey has found that more than 50% of small businesses do want government help, but struggle to find their way through the maze of provision. This means the businesses that will benefit most from such support are often those least likely to access it.

The Business Support Simplification Programme (BSSP) is streamlining the system by reducing the number of support schemes from more than 3,000 to less than 100. Business Link is now the single access point for small business advice in England. Businesses are directed to a range of private and public business support options through this central portal. The service is free, impartial and available nationally.

Furthermore, you could approach the National Federation of Enterprise Agencies (NFEA), which is a membership body for local enterprise agencies. It forms a network of independent agencies which can help small and growing businesses by providing a range of services, such as training and mentoring and providing loans, incubation and workspace. It operates through the nine UK regions and in turn has nine Regional Development Agencies.

NFEA's Small Business Advice Service (www.smallbusinessadvice.org.uk) provides free and confidential business advice and guidance to anyone planning to start up or run a small business. A feature of this service is the online Enquiry Service, which can link you directly to one of the 200 or more accredited business advisers. When you submit an enquiry, the service automatically routes it to the most appropriate adviser, based on your postcode. The registration process is simple: just fill in your email address, postcode and an indication of how you found the service. You are then allocated a 4-digit PIN number and to log in you just enter your email address and this PIN number. The service is totally confidential.

Together with Barclays Bank, the NFEA is also offering tailored pre-start-up support in each region. The programme is managed nationally by the NFEA and delivered locally by NFEA members with support from Barclays branches. The Let's Talk programme is made up of two elements:

☐ Business Ideas – a half-day event tailored to people in the early stages of deciding whether self-employment is for them.

☐ Starting a Business – a full-day event aimed at those who are almost ready to start their own business.

Its New Entrepreneur Scholarship programme also helps people from disadvantaged areas and backgrounds.

■ In England, the government has committed itself to the Business Link (www.businesslink.-gov.uk) as a gateway that small businesses can use to access a range of government services.

■ In Scotland, Scottish Enterprise (www.scottish-enterprise.com) and its local enterprise companies run Business Gateway (www.bgateway.com). They are both funded by the Scottish Executive and involve local councils, local enterprise trusts and other partners. For small businesses in the Highlands and Islands of Scotland, Highlands and Islands Enterprise (www.hie.co.uk) runs a similar service. Business Gateway offers assistance in helping small businesses access advice in many areas, including skills development, staff recruitment, sales and marketing, IT and the latest business regulations.

■ In Wales, the Welsh Assembly Government provides advice and support to businesses through a fully integrated service, Flexible Support for Business (www.business-support-wales.gov.uk). It allows fast, simple and straightforward access to information, with dedicated relationship managers, funding and specialist support.

■ In Northern Ireland, services for small businesses are provided by Invest NI (www.investni.com) and local enterprise agencies located in each of the council areas.

Applying for grants

Access to finance is critical to entrepreneurial success. It is important that businesses have the knowledge, skills and opportunities to access the finance they need to make their enterprising ideas a reality. For some, this will be about understanding what finance options there are to set up a business. For others, it will be about finding the right financial backing to help them realise their entrepreneurial ambition for business growth. Businesses also need to be able to access the support and advice they need to become investment-ready before they seek finance.

The UK's finance markets are arguably among the most flexible and dynamic in the world. Nevertheless, evidence suggests that, for a minority of businesses, barriers to accessing finance continue to exist. Over the last ten years the government has taken steps to support a more enabling environment for small businesses to gain better access to finance.

Despite this progress in improving access to debt and equity finance barriers still persist, with around 25,000 businesses a year with viable propositions unable to obtain the finance they require. Evidence also suggests that the proportion of small businesses obtaining no finance from the first source they try has increased from 9% to 13%. This may be through a combination of structural changes in the appraisal of bids for funding, the quality of businesses' propositions, and their presentation to lending institutions and potential investors. The business community believes that the challenge for government is to respond to the great demand for finance as a result of increased entrepreneurial activity, particularly younger businesses and those proposing to grow.

While the world of international finance and banking has been affected by the sub-prime lending problems in the USA, indications suggest that business banking has remained stable and that SME lending in the UK remains strong. However, the government is still committed to ensuring that businesses who are starting up and those seeking to expand and grow are not constrained in obtaining debt finance as a result of that financial market's disruption.

Getting grant funding could help your business develop but you must be ready to put up some of your own money. It is extremely rare for a grant to finance 100% of the costs of any project. Grants typically cover 15% to 50% of the total finance required. There are many different grant schemes in existence. You need to identify the specific grants your business or project could be eligible for.

Although many grants are available across most sectors, some sectors may be specifically targeted for extra funding. A lot of government support is targeted at growing businesses rather than one-man bands. Be aware that the criteria for qualifying businesses are often very specific and that grants may be limited to certain types of activity. Some grants are intended to help new businesses and boost employment. Local support (subsidised rent and rates) is often available to encourage small businesses to start up in particular areas.

Talk to the administrators of any grant schemes which seem to fit your situation. You must have a clear project plan: you will probably need to show how the project ties in with the strategic direction of your business as outlined in your business plan. It is probably worth paying for professional help to apply for any grants worth £50,000 or more. Experts can help you to model your project so that it is more likely to meet the qualifying criteria of the grant. Some accountants and consultants are grant experts.

Through the Small Firms Loan Guarantee (SFLG) the government has guaranteed more than 100,000 loans totalling £5 billion since 1981. This enables small businesses with a viable business plan, but lacking security, to borrow money from approved lenders. The SFLG is a joint venture between BERR and a number of participating lenders. A list of these lenders can be found at www.berr.gov.uk. These lenders administer the eligibility criteria and make all the commercial decisions regarding borrowing.

The main features are:

- A guarantee to the lender covering 75% of the loan amount; the borrower pays a 2% premium on the outstanding balance of the loan, payable quarterly by direct debit.

- It focuses on start-up and younger businesses who have been trading for less than five years.

- Loans of up to £250,000 are provided with terms of up to ten years.

- Availability is to qualifying UK businesses with an annual turnover of up to £5.6 million.

- It is open to businesses in most sectors and for most business purposes, although there are some restrictions.

As an additional incentive for investment in early stage and growth businesses, the government has used tax-based schemes through the Enterprise Investment Scheme (EIS) and Venture Capital Trusts (VCTs).

You should also contact your local Business Link or other business support organisations. Basic information is usually free. Most have access to the European Information Centre and to Grantfinder, a database which will identify the appropriate European, national and government grant schemes.

Business Link's Grants and Support Directory is an online database that you can search for potential sources of help, either at the start-up phase of your business or to assist you with further business development. It is an extensive database that includes information on grant and support schemes from central and local government as well as through private organisations.

www.j4bGRANTSco.uk gives comprehensive government grant information for the UK and Ireland and other sources of funding for your business. It has more than 4,500 financial programs researched with daily updates. Simply register for free and start searching.

Finding support and mentoring

There may be times when you will need specialist advice or to turn to people and organisations for support. There are many sources of information, advice and support available to people starting a new business. Business Link is the first place to look. Its service is delivered through advisers in your area, supported by a national website and a national phone line.

Enterprise agencies and chambers of commerce can also offer support. If you are aged 18 to 30, you might be able to get help from The Prince's Trust (www.princes-trust.org.uk), while the Prince's Initiative for Mature Enterprise (PRIME) at www.primeinitiative.org.uk helps the over-50s. Indeed, it is the only national organisation dedicated to helping people over 50. It offers a sympathetic ear, free information and help, workshops and business networking events.

A good accountant will tell you how to organise your business to make it as financially rewarding as possible. In addition, a reliable mentor will be an experienced and successful businessperson and a good listener. The online networking platform Horsesmouth (www.horsesmouth.co.uk) brings together those who have experience and those who are looking for answers. It's a kind of MySpace for business. More than likely you will not have a big management team, so it's good to have someone to speak to about things.

Recognising the value of business-to-business mentoring, the government says it will work with the Regional Development Agencies (RDAs) and leading private sector agencies to establish better links between existing mentoring programmes and the business support network overall.

You should also consider joining your trade association or getting involved in local and national small business organisations to help you build up your own network. Networking means speaking to other business people and this enables the sharing of ideas and experiences.

Women in business

While only 14% of small businesses with employees are led by women, the government has set up a £12.5 million fund to specifically encourage more women entrepreneurs. The new scheme will target mothers through children's centres and will offer advice on how to prepare business plans, how to run a firm, and how to pitch for investment. Contact BERR (www.berr.gov.uk) for more information.

4
ASSESSING YOUR COSTS

Working out how much your start-up costs are likely to be will help you to stay in control of your finances right from the beginning. You will also be able to work out if you can spread your start-up costs or you may be able to identify those areas where you can reduce your spending.

You will have to make some big purchases, such as equipment, and at first it might be wise to lease such items. You will need to stock up and without a trade history, you may have to pay for goods up front. If you rent premises, the landlord will expect a deposit and rent in advance. You might also have to fit out, decorate, or upgrade the building and service charges will have to be paid.

On top of all this, there will be telephone and utility bills to pay, as well as tax, insurance, business rates and a range of other overheads. There may also be interest to pay on bank loans. Finally you will have to think about how much you are going to pay people each month – and don't forget to include your own wages.

Shopping around for insurance

When starting your business, do shop around for the cheapest insurance quotes. Don't accept the first offer as this could end up costing you more than necessary in the long run. Work out the cover you need and then compare quotes because you may well find a better deal. Costs are continually rising and can chip away at the profits of independent shops. Businesses who do not consider their insurance carefully risk having inadequate cover, thus leaving them open to the threat of being unable to recoup their losses in the event of fire, theft, or damage. As well as trusted providers there are other insurance companies which can offer savings on comprehensive policies.

Some insurances are compulsory and others should be considered on their merits. You are required to have employers' liability insurance if you decide to employ staff. This covers the cost of claims and legal fees if an employee becomes ill or is injured at work as a result of what they do for you. By law your insurance must cover at least £5 million, but most policies will offer at least £10 million.

If you use a motor vehicle for business purposes, you are required to have third party motor insurance. It must cover a minimum of £1 million for property damage and a further unlimited amount for personal injury.

Other insurance products which are not required by law include protection against the risk of compensation claims and legal action; protection for your premises, goods in transit, freezer breakdown, business interruption, public liability, and for your employees; and protection against financial risk. Often shop owners will buy a loss of licence insurance.

Some insurers do deal directly with businesses or alternatively you can buy your insurance through a broker or a trade association, which may have links to insurers who specialise in the food retail trade. If you opt for an insurance broker, approach three different brokers and ask them all to make recommendations for you.

You can check if the organisation or person you deal with is authorised by looking at the Financial Services Authority's site at www.fsa.gov.uk. Members of The Guild of Fine Food, (www.finefoodworld.co.uk) benefit from preferential rates on a shop insurance package.

Answer all the questions fully and disclose all the relevant facts concerning your business when completing the proposal form. Failure to do so may entitle the insurer to treat the policy as invalid. Your insurer will help you work out what level of cover you need. You can either pay a lump sum or you can spread the costs by paying a smaller amount each month. Be sure to check the interest rate charged. You may also be able to save money by buying cover that lasts for more than a year.

More information is available from the British Insurance Brokers' Association at www.biba.org.uk, the Financial Ombudsman Service (FOS) at www.financial-ombudsman.org.uk, and the Institute of Insurance Brokers (IIB) at www.iib-uk.com.

Covering rent, rates and utilities

The cost of rents can vary enormously. If you have not yet decided on a particular premises, contact a local estate agent who handles commercial property to get an idea of how much the rent is likely to be. You should have already given some consideration to the type and location of the business premises that you will require, so they will be able to give you some guidance as to how much you will have to pay. Your solicitor will help you with the lease agreement but make sure that you are clear about how frequently the rent will be reviewed, how long the lease runs for, and what you and your landlord are each responsible for. Bear in mind your premises should be accessible to those customers who are disabled.

RATES

Business rates are a contentious issue for small business and are often the third largest expenditure item after wages and rent. If you use a building or part of a building for your business, you will probably have to pay business rates. When you start a new business or move into new premises, you should tell the local council so they can charge you the correct amount.

The amount of business rates payable is calculated using the rateable value and a multiplier, which is set by the government. In England, the standard multiplier for 2008/09 is 46.2 (different multipliers are used for Wales, Scotland and Northern Ireland).

So, if your property has a rateable value of £10,000 it will be charged at £4,620. The rateable value is based on the likely annual open market rent for the premises at a particular date. Rateable values are reviewed every five years and were last updated on 1 April 2005.

Different parts of the premises may be valued at different levels. For example, the front part of a shop, nearest the entrance, is more valuable than space further back or storage space in the basement.

In England and Wales, small business are entitled to small business rate relief if the rateable value of the premises is less than £15,000 (£21,500 in London). In Northern Ireland, there is a hardship relief scheme for small businesses which came into operation on 31 December 2005. Certain rural businesses may also be able to claim rate relief.

Business ratepayers who are eligible have to apply for this relief each year. You have to send the relevant application to your local authority within six months of the end of the financial year to which the relief applies.

Certain businesses in the countryside can also qualify, such as those in small villages with a population under 3,000. You can qualify for a 50% reduction in the rates bill if you are the only general store in a village.

If the rateable value of your premises has increased, the maximum account your bill can increase by is 15% in 2008/09; if it decreases then your bill will decrease by 60%. Details of the rateable value of your premises and how it has been calculated can be viewed at the Valuation Office Agency (VOA) at www.voa.gov.uk and the Scottish Assessors Association (SAA) at www.saa.gov.uk.

There are moves to relocalise business rates which are being opposed by the Federation of Small Businesses. The FSB believes a system of locally set business rates will be detrimental to small businesses, resulting in higher and less predictable business rate bills. Therefore the FSB is lobbying government for a reduction in the level of business rates and, at a local level, to persuade councils to help reduce the financial burden that small businesses face.

This is a huge burden placed on any small business; the rates bill will be on average three times greater than for a larger business. With the prospect of business rate supplements, workplace parking levies, congestion charging and, in some cases, business improvement district levies, today's businesses are overwhelmed with charges, levies and taxes, says the FSB:

> *Local authorities need to recognise the enormous contribution small businesses make to the economic sustainability of a community and help them wherever they can. Local authorities must also do more to promote the Small Business Rate Relief scheme which many small businesses are unaware they are eligible for.*

The FSB believes that business rate relief should be automatic for small businesses, with no need to engage in any application procedure. Additionally, many businesses do not know that councils have the power to reduce or remit all or part of a business rates bill on the grounds that the ratepayer is in extreme financial hardship.

UTILITIES

Until you have been trading for a few months you will not know exactly how much gas and electricity your deli will use. Your energy supplier may be able to give you some guidance, based on the size of your premises and the nature of any equipment you will be using (for example, commercial cookers, freezers and fridges). You can adjust the figures once you have been in the premises for a few months.

You will be billed every quarter. All the utility companies have become much more competitive, so it might be worth shopping around to see which would be the cheapest for your energy needs.

TELEPHONES

Your business will need at least one telephone line to contact suppliers, take customers' orders and handle general enquiries. You may also decide that you need a fax machine. It's important to have internet access – ideally broadband – and an email address.

The luxury of negotiating bulk telephone rates is not available to small players, so keeping your costs down can be an uphill struggle. However, voice over internet protocol (VoIP) – a technology that allows you to make calls using a broadband connection instead of an analogue phone line – can save you money on telephone bills.

According to studies recently released, more than 60% of small firms in the UK spend in excess of £300 a month on fixed line calls and £400 a month on mobile phone calls. Research also shows that small- and medium-sized enterprises (SMEs) that switched over to VoIP experienced on average a 23% reduction in overheads and a 13% fall in IT expenses.

Popular UK providers that can meet the internet telephony needs of a small business include Skype, Call Union, PlusTalk, Vonage and Tesco. The greatest benefit of using these packages is that, where two locations are equipped with the same service, the calls are free.

The initial charges will vary according to the provider, but Vonage currently charges £7.99 monthly rental with a £9.99 set-up fee and £8.99 for equipment delivery. Calls are free to all landlines in the UK and Ireland. With Skype you would currently pay £2.24 monthly subscription with calls to landlines in the UK and Ireland charged at about 1p per minute. You can buy a USB cordless phone for less than £15 and also have incoming Skype calls forwarded to your mobile phone.

A standard BT landline (not a VoIP service) today costs £10.50 a month plus £124.99 for installation of the phone line. Call charges will vary depending on your payment plan. You will be billed every quarter for the calls you have made, plus an extra amount for the line rental for the next quarter.

BROADBAND

A reliable business broadband service is invaluable when running a small business. It offers faster download speeds and support. However, an unreliable connection can cost valuable time and money.

Most business broadband providers will offer a free domain name and a static Internet Protocol (IP) address. A domain name allows you to create your own name which will help you build both credibility and market awareness. A static IP address also allows you to access your PC from anywhere in the country and to run your own email server, web server and private network.

A typical package, such as UK Online's Business Broadband Package (www.ukonline.net) will cost from £19.99 a month (plus VAT) and will come with a free connection for a limited period. It has an 8Mb connection; unlimited service; a UK-based 24/7 freephone for technical support; up to 20 email addresses with a domain name, webmail and spam filter; and free McAfee Security for 12 months.

OTHER GENERAL EXPENSES

Every month you are likely to spend some money on different things for your business. This will include:

- **Business stationery** Letterheads, business cards, invoices and other miscellaneous stationery items are important for the image and efficiency of your deli. Your local printer will be able to give you an estimate on how much each of these will cost.

- **Postage** You are likely to spend a certain amount on a regular basis, but every now and then you might decide to do a mail shot advertising your business.

- **Window cleaner** You may wish to have your windows cleaned daily or maybe just once or twice a week.

- **Repairs and maintenance** Take out a contract with a plumber, electrician and heating engineer. It could save you money in the long run. Furthermore, for advice on structure and repairs use a qualified surveyor who is a member of the Royal Institution of Chartered Surveyors (www.rics.org).

- **Membership of a trade association** To join The Guild of Fine Food costs £105.75 annually. This includes copies of the *Fine Food Digest*. (For other trade publications see 'Trade Publications and Websites' at the end of this book.)

- **Subscription to a trade journal** Non-members will pay £40 a year for ten issues of *Fine Food Digest*.

Stocking up

Some considerable thought should go into the type of products you are going to stock. Once you have decided on your product base, pick out suppliers you believe can offer the quality of product and service you need. To work out your initial costs, ask your selected suppliers to send product details, price lists and other relevant information. Don't be afraid to shop around for the best deals. Reliability, quality, service and value for money should all be taken into consideration when choosing suppliers.

Get a number of quotes, including details like discounts and payment terms. Ask how often prices will rise, what influences will cause them to rise, and how you will be notified. Specify what you want and agree the details, proposing your own terms. But don't be tempted to squeeze a supplier if you plan to buy regularly from that source.

By building a good relationship with your suppliers, you will save money and time in the long run. It may even improve the quality of the goods you receive. Understand how your suppliers work and discuss with them whether a contract or service level agreement (SLA) is necessary. A guide to purchasing strategies, including improving supplier quality and reliability, removing risk and saving yourself time and money, is available from the Buying Support Agency at www.buyingsupport.co.uk.

Says Gary Williamson, of Corner on the Square deli in Inverness:

There are plenty of wholesalers and producers looking for business. It is important to share your goals with them and find those that are willing to be part of your business and to share in any success.

Agree your payment terms so there are no disputes in the future. Payment in advance should generally be avoided, especially if you are unsure about the supplier's creditworthiness. For convenience, it's best to set up accounts with your main suppliers. Ask for a discount for early settlement, retrospective rebates, or volume discounts. Remember, holding stock ties up money, so aim to minimise your stock levels and to make delivery of supplies the supplier's responsibility. The Law Society (www.lawsociety.org.uk) has useful information on contracts with suppliers on their website.

Make your delivery terms clear when you place the contract. Always check what has actually been delivered before you sign the delivery note. For small delis, a weekly stock check and ordering routine should be sufficient. Devise your own system but keep accurate records of all purchases.

Suppliers are easy enough to find but do spend time on research. You can then ask around, check with the trade associations, look at trade journals, enquire at your local Chamber of Commerce and Business Link, visit exhibitions and trade fairs and browse through directories, such as www.yell.com, www.thelocalweb.net or www.scoot.co.uk. (Also see Chapter 7.)

Employing and managing staff

I'm lucky I have fantastic people working with me. One of the most difficult things is to get good people, train them, progress them and keep it stabilised. They have to learn about hundreds of product lines to be able to advise customers correctly. I now have 15 to 18 staff members who work on a steady basis and most of them were found by putting an advert in the shop window.

So says Fi Buchanan, of Heart Buchanan Fine Food & Wine in Glasgow. However, deciding when to take on an employee is a balancing act. Firstly, you may not be able to cover the increased costs straightaway but, on the other hand, it may free up your time to take on other activities to increase your profits.

Before you employ someone, examine the sort of skills and knowledge the person will need for the job and the amount of time they may need to work on their own initiative. Determine the working hours and the wage you will offer. Set up a recruitment procedure and be clear about what descriptions and questions are legally unacceptable in job advertisements and interviews. Work out a simple application form for candidates to fill in before you see them.

You may need staff to:

- ☐ Choose and buy stock (if you won't be doing this yourself).

- ☐ Monitor stock.

- ☐ Receive deliveries.

- ☐ Answer the telephone.

- ☐ Price items.

- ☐ Contact trade customers.

- ☐ Take orders if you have a take-away or eat-in service.

- ☐ Make up dishes.

- ☐ Slice meat and other products.

- ☐ Display products and make sure they are kept clean and appealing.

- ☐ Serve and advise customers.

- ☐ Make sandwiches for the lunch-time trade.

- ☐ Organise tastings and promotions.

- ☐ Keep the business records.

- ☐ Make deliveries.

If you have a licence to sell alcohol your staff must be conversant with licensing legislation. Training will be necessary to make sure your staff know why and how a job has to be done. There are number of ways in which you could recruit new employees:

- ☐ By advertising locally or in speciality publications.

- ☐ By writing to colleges and schools for candidates.

- ☐ By contacting the job centre.

- ☐ By using employment agencies.

Job centres give their services free, but an employment agency could cost you as much as 20% of the employee's first year's salary. When interviewing, give candidates exact written details of the job description and inform all applicants once you have made a decision.

As soon as you take someone on, you should draw up a contract of employment as this will prevent any disputes arising. By law (the Employment Rights Act), all employees are entitled to receive a written statement of employment from their employer within two months of starting work. Written particulars have to be included to break down or explain in detail the terms and conditions of employment. By law you are required to provide these details to your employee.

The following details should be included:

- ☐ Names of the employer and employee.

- ☐ The date employment started.

- ☐ A job title and a brief description of the main duties.

- ☐ The address where the employee will be working.

- ☐ The scale or rate of pay.

- ☐ At what intervals the employee will be paid (weekly, monthly).

- ☐ The employee's working hours.

- ☐ The employee's holiday entitlement.

- ☐ The terms relating to injury, sickness, and sick pay.

- ☐ The period of employment.

- ☐ All pension details.

- ☐ The disciplinary and grievance procedures.

- ☐ Whether the job is full-time, part-time, temporary or contractual.

- ☐ The length of notice required.

- ☐ A clause that will allow you to end the contract after a trial period.

- ☐ Collective agreements (trade unions).

It is against the law to discriminate against candidates because of their disability, race, colour, nationality, ethnic origins, sex or marital status. Make sure you are working within health and safety regulations and that you understand fully the rules about dismissing an employee.

You can get advice about drawing up a written contract from Acas (www.acas.org.uk), your solicitor, or the local business support organisation. Free leaflets, published by BERR, are also available from your local JobCentre Plus.

Maintaining accurate and up-to-date staff details is a prerequisite for all your dealings with employees. The better you treat them, the better they will treat you. Show your appreciation for a job well done. You could set targets with a bonus incentive. Always pay wages on time and at competitive rates.

The current national minimum wage is £5.52 an hour, £4.60 for 18 to 21 year olds and £3.40 for 16 to 17 year olds. If you have five or more staff, you must provide access to a stakeholder pension scheme. You must deduct tax and national insurance contributions from your employees' wages and pay these to HMRC.

The wages you pay your staff will depend to some extent on what is the going rate in your area. The *Annual Survey of Hours and Earnings*, carried out by the government, gives average weekly wages for a wide range of different types of job. The survey is available online at www.statistics.gov.

If you employ anyone, full- or part-time, aged 16 or over, who does not have leave to enter or remain in the UK and/or who is not entitled to work here, it is a criminal offence. There are 13 types of documents that are acceptable as proof of entitlement. They include a documented P45, a P60, a birth certificate issued within the UK or the Republic of Ireland, a work permit, or a British passport showing that the holder has the right of abode or re-admission to the UK. Protect yourself by asking to see one of these. Temporary national insurance numbers are not acceptable.

Mostly we have found the right staff but we always seem to be short of someone. As a seasonal business it can be tricky on the shoulder periods, such as late summer, when the university students who have helped you through the busy summer period return to uni and you have a shop full of customers! Flexibility as an employer is the key to retailing staff, this can be an onerous task often leading to you changing your plans rather than the employee.

So says Gary Williamson, of the Corner on the Square deli in Inverness.

Keeping employees happy is the most obvious way to retain staff. Get to know your staff, their personalities and personal circumstances as far as you can. Giving praise for a job well done and offering rewards and perks can make a big difference. Staff will also appreciate taking on new tasks and responsibilities so try to create new opportunities for their further development. Sending someone to an exhibition or a new training course may reap rewards. Communicate properly with your staff and show an interest in them. Finally, if you find you have to discipline a member of staff, make sure the process is fair.

Buying the right equipment

Costs for equipping your deli will depend on the size and location of your premises. If food is prepared on site, this will affect the range and type of equipment you will have to buy to comply with health and safety legislation. The following equipment applies to a small delicatessen and to those intending to prepare cold foods on site.

☐ Refrigerated glass display counter/unit – from £1,060.

☐ Glass door upright freezer – from £719.

- ☐ Bottle cooler – from £265.

- ☐ Large fridges and freezers – from £892 separately.

- ☐ Serve over display – from £939.

- ☐ Stainless steel work (wall) benches – from £119.

- ☐ Base cabinets – from £540.

- ☐ Wall units – from £431.

- ☐ Wash basins – from £105.

- ☐ Coffee machines – from £189.

- ☐ Professional juicer – from £299.

- ☐ Professional food processor and blender – from £413.

- ☐ Non-porous food preparation surfaces – from £150 each.

- ☐ Large marble cheese slabs with glass dome – from £120.

- ☐ Scales with stainless steel measuring bowl – from £50.

- ☐ Food slicer – from £458.

- ☐ Vegetable cutter – £610.

- ☐ Cash tills - from £400.

Miscellaneous equipment will include knives (from £70), chopping boards (from £12), and insect control (from £30). You will need to buy shelving and paper or plastic bags. You should also obviously budget for stocking your shop with the products you intend to sell.

In addition to the other services it offers, the Heart of England Fine Foods food group (www.heff.co.uk) runs a Savour the Flavour branded retail scheme whereby member retail outlets receive a branded fridge, freezer or shelving unit for a small handling fee if they pledge to purchase goods from food and drink producers in the region. If you list six new producers you will receive a unit worth up to the value of £500; 12 new producers gives you a unit or units worth up to £1,000; and for 18 new producers you will be delivered units up to the value of £1,500.

In general, gather together enough information to put together a realistic life-cycle costing. When buying new equipment calculate the purchase price, any interest on loan charges, full running costs and the maintenance costs. Do this calculation for a five-year period, divide the total by 260, and it will give you the weekly profit required.

Be careful when buying equipment as part of the purchase of premises, especially when taking over leased equipment. Check the exact terms of the lease and make sure all the equipment is transferred into your name.

When buying or leasing equipment, think carefully about the following:

☐ Technical specifications.

☐ Compatibility with other equipment.

☐ Power supply.

☐ Guarantees.

☐ Technical support.

☐ Options for expansion and upgrading.

☐ Purchase price.

☐ Delivery and installation costs.

☐ Maintenance costs.

☐ Running costs.

Be careful of lengthy maintenance contracts. Read the small print carefully and ask your supplier to explain your present and future commitments.

You may decide to lease some items and one advantage of a leasing agreement is that the cost can be spread over a set period, which will help your cash flow. Generally, the payments will be fixed at the beginning of the lease period and paid monthly. Ownership of the equipment remains with the leasing company, although you will more than likely be responsible for the maintenance. Your equipment supplier may offer leasing facilities, but if not contact the Finance and Leasing Association (www.fla.org.uk) who will give you a list of those that do.

Food hygiene regulations make clean, new equipment of the utmost importance. It is the retailer's responsibility to ensure that all goods are stored and displayed at the correct temperature. Unless your equipment was made in the last few years, it is unlikely to perform to these regulations.

Older equipment is usually difficult to modify due to incorrect sizing of compressors and air flows and the lack of a defrost facility. In addition, older equipment is likely to contain CFC refrigerants, which were phased out of the UK in 1994. Care should also be taken when considering what size of equipment to buy. A smaller cabinet may be better, particularly if your stock will be concentrated on faster selling premium lines.

Keep a daily check on your refrigeration equipment. Your chilled display cabinets should run cooler than the minimum requirement for the core temperature of certain foods and that is 5° C. Regular temperature testing of the food will tell you if your equipment is working within the law.

New refrigeration equipment is likely to have higher running costs but you should be able to control these. Ventilation is one of the most important factors in this regard. Heat given off by equipment can build, particularly at night when your premises are closed. There are two ways of overcoming this:

☐ Cabinets can be positioned against an outer wall with grills behind the unit to allow the hot air to escape.

☐ You can install a suitably sized ventilation fan controlled by a thermostat. This will ensure a gentle passage of air throughout the shop to the benefit of all concerned. Avoid excessive draughts across the front of the refrigerated display cabinets. Advice should be obtained from your local contractor.

Always remember that service checks save money in the long run and maintenance contracts are the best option.

5
DEALING WITH TAXATION

According to the Federation of Small Business (FSB), it is widely acknowledged that tax legislation has become increasingly complex over the last decade and small businesses, without access to expensive auditors, are the ones paying the price. The constant changes to the tax regime and tax changes also make any long-term strategic business plans very difficult. What small businesses want, above all, is simplification and stability.

Says John Wright, National Chairman of the FSB:

> *The government's approach to the taxation of small businesses remains alarmingly disjointed and inconsistent. For several years, the business community has been waiting for the outcome of the government's small business tax policy review. Instead, what has been received is a never-ending raft of badly thought through last-minute measures, designed to tackle problems in one part of the taxation regime, but ending up creating several more somewhere else.*
>
> *The notion that the government is 'consulting' with the small business sector on tax policy remains fictional. It is extremely disappointing to see that again and again, the interests of the small business sector are ignored in favour of big business and unsubstantial claims of non-compliant small business.*
>
> *Although the proposal on capital gains tax has now been revisited, the initial proposal demonstrated just how poor the government's understanding of the small business sector really is. Similarly with the increase in the small firms' corporation tax rate and the proposed draconian legislation on income shifting, the government has displayed huge ignorance of the challenges that small businesses face.*

Relationship with HMRC

The FSB also believes that there is a fundamental lack of understanding in HM Revenue & Customs (HMRC) about how small businesses operate and that this knowledge gap needs to be tackled. Although the FSB is encouraged by some of the work currently being driven by HMRC, concerns remain that small businesses' needs are still often overlooked in the consultation process.

The move towards using call centres and closing local tax offices has been detrimental to small businesses's relationship with HMRC. The FSB has urged the government to review the inspection regime for small businesses. Many small businesses find enquiries and inspections extremely intrusive and costly, and disproportionately heavy-handed to the amount of extra revenue raised.

Says Angus Ferguson, of Demijohn deli in Edinburgh and Glasgow:

Red tape or bureaucracy should not put anyone off wishing to get started. Ultimately, there will be a time when you will need to tick all the boxes on the list of administrative procedures, but there is time to do that once you are up and running. As long as you know what you will eventually need to do to fulfil all the legal requirements for being in business, just get started.

Record-keeping and taxes

Keeping accurate records of your business accounting activities is vital. As well as giving you an idea of how well your business is doing, without proper records you could end up paying the wrong amount of tax.

It is a legal requirement and self-assessment relies on it. You must register with the HMRC within the first three months, even if you already use a self-assessment tax return. There are penalties for not registering.

You need to keep the following records:

- A cash book – keeping track of all your financial incomings and outgoings.

- A sales ledger – recording any invoices you may have sent out.

- A purchase ledger – recording any money you owe to other companies.

- A petty cash book – keeping account of all your miscellaneous spending.

Keep your receipts, bank statements and building society books. When dealing with cash, you will need till receipts and a record book to keep track of it all. Try and keep records of your pricing policy as this will affect the overall gross profit rate of your business. HMRC will look at your trading results to see if your gross profit is in line with industry norms.

You are responsible for the entries you make on your tax return, and if HMRC have any queries you will need to go back to your records. Bank statements, receipts and cash transaction records are all essential for working out your profits for the year and HMRC uses this information to calculate your tax and national insurance.

The tax year runs from 6 April to 5 April. Tax is due in two equal instalments: on January 31 (during that tax year), and July 31 (after the end of the tax year). These interim payments are based on the previous year's tax liability. A balancing payment is due on the following January 31, to adjust the difference between the amounts paid and the tax due as a result of actual profits.

National Insurance (NI) is a contribution towards state benefits, such as retirement pension, unemployment and incapacity benefits. If you employ staff you must make sure that employers' and employees' NI contributions are paid. There are four different types of national insurance which are applied according to status:

☐ Class 1 NICs are payable by anyone who is employed. They are a percentage of your earnings above a certain threshold. Employers deduct Class 1 NICs automatically, along with PAYE income tax.

☐ Class 2 NICs are payable by anyone who is self-employed. It is a fixed weekly amount, paid by direct debit or quarterly bill. If earnings are below £4,635 a year, you may be entitled to an exemption or a refund.

☐ Class 3 NICs are voluntary. They cover shortfalls in your National Insurance contribution record and help protect your entitlement to a state pension and bereavement benefits.

☐ Class 4 NICs are payable by self-employed people. They are currently 8% of your annual taxable profit from self-employment, but you will only start paying Class 4 when your profits reach a certain limit (between £5,225 and £34,840). You include Class 4 on your tax return.

☐ **Sole traders** This means that you are an individual who is self-employed. There are two types of National Insurance for the self-employed: Class 2 and Class 4. The self-employed pay less NI than employees, but in return they receive significantly fewer benefits. VAT is payable if you reach the registration threshold.

- **Partnership** Each partner pays income tax, through the self-assessment system, as well as Class 2 and Class 4 National Insurance. The business itself also pays VAT once you reach the registration threshold.

- **Limited company** If you set up a limited company (and therefore an employee) you will pay tax on your income every time you are paid. This is called PAYE (Pay as You Earn). You have to deduct tax and NICs from your salary through your company's payroll, which you have to set up. Your business also has to pay employers' NICs for its employees. Company directors need to file statutory documents, such as accounts and annual returns.

There is also corporation tax to think about, which is charged on company profits. Companies have to calculate their own corporation tax and then make a payment to HMRC. A tax rate of 20% applies to small businesses with a taxable profit of up to £300,000. Companies with profits of more than £1.5m pay corporation tax in quarterly instalments, while other companies pay nine months after the accounting year-end.

When you are calculating profits, remember HMRC has strict rules on what can be counted as a business expense. Allowable expenses include: rent and the running costs for premises; the cost of goods bought as stock and then resold; the financing and marketing costs. Costs that are not allowed include: personal expenses (travel to work); living expenses or clothes; money spent entertaining clients; and fines (parking tickets).

When working out your profits, you cannot count the cost of purchasing premises and equipment as an expense. You will need to claim capital allowance on these, which allows you to deduct a proportion of the cost from your taxable profit over several years.

The allowance is calculated as a fixed percentage of an item's value each year. Capital allowances range from 4% to 100%, depending on your type of business and what you are buying. Capital Gains Tax (CGT) is a tax on successful investment (property, shares, or the sale of a business). If you sell something for more than you paid for it, CGT might be payable. CGT will not usually be payable on the sale of your home (although you could end up paying some if you claim some of your mortgage payments as a business expense).

Limited companies pay corporation tax on capital gains, because these are treated as part of the company's taxable profit. Self-employed people pay CGT at their top rate of income tax. There are allowances and exemptions.

Provided you have informed HMRC that you have started your business, you can claim expenses incurred before you started trading as allowable expenses in your first year. There are exceptions, such as training courses and the cost of forming a limited company. Solicitors or accountants will be able to offer advice on all of this.

Records must be kept for six years. Your accountant will be able to give you advice on how best to keep records. You might decide to go for a computerised system, which will help your accountant to draw up your accounts at the end of the year. Bookkeeping isn't just a means of satisfying the tax man, it can tell you how well your business is performing, how you could cut costs, and which of your customers are buying from you the most. Neglecting it means your accountant will take longer to draw up your accounts and in the long run this will cost you money.

Any HMRC office will be able to let you have a copy of *Self-Assessment: A General Guide to Keeping Records*, or a leaflet on corporation tax.

Value added tax explained

VAT is a transaction tax on sales of goods and services. If your business sells products or services at a total value worth more than the amount set by the government, VAT registration is compulsory. This threshold is currently £67,000.

The VAT you charge (17.5% on the goods you sell) is known as output tax. You will be able to reclaim any VAT you pay on goods and services purchased for your business. This is input tax.

It is the difference between the two (output tax minus input tax) that you pay to HMRC. It's normally collected four times a year. However, if you paid more VAT than you have charged, you will be due a refund.

There are detailed and complicated regulations surrounding VAT, including different rates for various types of products or services and when exactly the tax has to be paid. You will likely sell a mixture of standard-rated and zero-rated items.

Zero-rated items include:
Cold take-away food and sandwiches
Culinary herbs
Cereals, nuts and pulses
Bread, rolls, baps and pittas
Flapjacks
Milk, coconut milk
Tea, coffee
Vegetables and fruit

Standard rated items include:
Hot take-away food
Alcoholic drinks
Soft drinks
Juice and juice concentrates
Confectionery
Ice cream
Potato crisps, roasted and salted nuts
Ornamental vegetables

Your suppliers will be able to guide you on this as many invoices will show whether an item is zero- or standard-rated. Otherwise refer to HMRC's *VAT Notice 701/14, Food*.

Fines for late payment or procedural failures can be severe. If need be, seek advice from an accountant. HMRC also produces a wide range of helpful information, including *Should I Be Registered for VAT?* You can also download other useful forms and publications.

The alternative flat rate scheme

You might be interested in an optional flat rate scheme (FRS) that operates for eligible small businesses. Under this scheme you will continue to issue tax invoices to VAT-registered customers, but the VAT payable every quarter is calculated as a percentage of your VAT-inclusive turnover. You will therefore apply the appropriate flat rate percentage for your type of business. This scheme cannot be used with the retail schemes or the cash accounting scheme. Full details of the FRS can be found in *Notice 700/1 Flat Rate Scheme for Small Businesses*. It will help you to decide whether or not the scheme is suitable for you.

Choosing good advisers

FINDING AN ACCOUNTANT

The right time to seek out professional help comes fairly early in the planning stage. Good advisers, usually an accountant and a solicitor, are vital when dealing with complex business issues. If you choose poorly you may find that your business suffers because someone is not keeping you properly informed.

An accountant should be recruited during the planning phase. Receiving advice from the start can prevent problems in the future. Accountancy firms offer a wide range of business services, including what form the business should take, bookkeeping, drawing up the annual accounts, preparing tax and VAT returns, handling the operation of PAYE, giving tax and business advice and so on.

Here are a few ways to track down the right accountant:

☐ Ask your business friends and colleagues.

☐ Speak to your bank manager or solicitor.

☐ Contact your local business support organisation, Chamber of Commerce, or Business Link.

☐ Look in the local papers and trade magazines.

☐ The *Yellow Pages* and *Thomson Local* directories also publish lists of accountants and Search Accountant (www.searchaccountant.co.uk) has a directory of UK accountants.

There are also several organisations that regulate the accountancy profession. Members of these organisations are professionally qualified and are bound to uphold the business ethics their organisations maintain. They are:

☐ The Institute of Chartered Accountants in England and Wales (ICAEW) at www.icaew.co.uk

☐ The Association of Chartered Accountants (ACCA) at www.accaglobal.com

☐ The Institute of Chartered Accounts of Scotland (ICAS) at www.icas.org.uk

Prepare a shortlist with a minimum of two and a maximum of six practices that you want to call. Ask them for information about their size, specialisation and experience. Basically, you want an accountant who specialises in small business work. Request an informal first meeting with no charge.

Before committing yourself, check on the estimated fees and billing arrangements. You should not be afraid to question and negotiate fees. Quite often the first-year fees will be competitively low and will then increase steeply in the second year. Some firms will want you to pay on a monthly basis, others may choose to do the work and then bill you when your accounts are produced.

One alternative is to use the free advice offered by your local support agency.

FINDING A SOLICITOR

There are different types of law and solicitors who specialise in certain areas. The Law Society operates a scheme called Lawyers for Your Business (LFYB), a network of

1,200 legal firms offering specialist advice to small- and medium-sized businesses. Solicitors will give an initial free consultation when you are starting up, running or growing your business. Thereafter, remember to ask for an estimate of costs or their daily rate.

A directory of legal firms and individual solicitors that are affiliated to the Law Society can be found at www.solicitors-online.com and can be searched by name, specialisation and area. Solicitors UK (www.solicitors-uk.org.uk) has a directory of UK solicitors and at Lawyer Locator (www.lawyerlocator.co.uk) you can find a local solicitor or law firm in your area. As well as using an online directory service, recommendations from other companies or business associates, such as your bank manager or accountant, are a good way to start.

6
BUYING AN EXISTING DELI

If you are concerned about starting from scratch, you might think about buying an up-and-running deli. The first step would be to get professional advice before you make any commitment. Then speak to the departing owners about their reasons for selling and have a long look at their trading history.

Buying a going concern

Buying a going concern means that the premises, business equipment and shop fittings are already in place; there are established customers; the business can generate income immediately; suppliers have been identified and relationships established with them; and the business has a track record, which can help if you are looking for finance.

The price of a delicatessen will depend on where the business is located, the quality of its fixtures and fittings, how successful it is and whether you are buying a freehold or a leasehold business.

Your market research into locality will help you to establish whether or not the owner is selling because he or she can no longer generate enough income from the business. This may not necessarily act as a deterrent: you may feel confident about turning a failing business around.

Check the state of the premises, its fittings and equipment and decide whether you will have to spend money on refurbishing or replacing assets. Consider the condition and value of the stock you are buying and verify that all products are within their sell-by dates.

A freehold will include the value of the building and the commercial value of the business and its fixtures and fittings. A leasehold means paying for the business, fixtures and fittings, the existing goodwill and the right to occupy the premises for the length of the lease.

Register your interest in buying the deli with the professional adviser who is normally employed to sell up. Ensure there are no problems with the business and complete a preliminary due diligence before you make a firm offer. Evaluate any key risks that may be associated with future trading. If after this you are still interested, obtain professional advice to help you value the business.

Choose advisers with the appropriate experience who can also assist in analysing any historical information and trends. Calculate your initial offer and your maximum offer and then submit it. Set out the payment structure and complete a legal due diligence. As soon as the deal is completed announce the change of ownership in a positive way.

To find a deli for sale, look in your local newspapers or associated magazines. Daltons, the business for sale website (www.daltonbusiness.com) which is part of *Daltons Weekly* has a range of delis for sale. Business transfer agents and estate agents concerned with retail businesses can also be helpful. In addition, check out the following online business seller: www.nationwidebusinesses.co.uk/Business/Delicatessens-for-sale.aspx

EXAMPLES OF DELIS FOR SALE
Here are a few that are typical:

Delicatessen for Sale, South London
Secure lease, fixtures and fittings
Price £75,000
Turnover £3,500 a week
Gross Profit 40%

Well Established Delicatessen for Sale, Lincolnshire
Freehold, fixtures and fittings
Price £215,000
Turnover £1,800 a week
Gross profit 45%

Leasehold Delicatessen for Sale, East Sussex
Owners retiring
Price £39,995
Turnover £2,400 a week
Gross Profit 33%

Franchising pros and cons

If you want to run your own deli but at the same time keep risk to a minimum, you may wish to buy into a franchise. It is generally held that successful franchise operations have a much lower failure rate than completely new businesses. It also means you don't have to start from scratch.

A franchise is the legal arrangement where the franchisor gives permission for the franchisee to use its name, brand, product, trade mark, operation and service in return for payment. Franchised businesses are more likely to succeed than many other start-ups because they will have a proven track record as well as established and effective processes in place.

The advantages of taking up a franchise are:

☐ Market knowledge.

☐ Innovation.

☐ Access to a successful business formula.

☐ A national advertising campaign and a recognised brand name.

☐ Support and training programmes in sales and all business skills.

☐ Help with securing funding for your investment, as well as discounted bulk-buy supplies for outlets when you are in operation.

The drawbacks include:

☐ The cost may be too high: you will pay an initial fee (often between £5,000 to £10,000, but as much as £250,000) to buy into a franchise.

☐ Paying an ongoing royalty on sales whether you are making a profit or not.

☐ No flexibility.

☐ Higher risks that are out of your control.

☐ The franchise doesn't deliver.

According to the British Franchise Association (BFA) at www.thebfa.org customers will understand that you will be offering the best possible value for money and service but that while you run your 'own show' you are part of a much larger organisation.

Each business outlet is owned and operated by the franchisee. However, the franchisor retains control over the way in which products and services are marketed and sold, and controls the quality and standards of the business.

The franchisor will receive an initial fee from the franchisee, payable at the outset, together with on-going management service fees, usually based on a percentage of annual turnover or the mark-ups on supplies. In return, the franchisor has an obligation to support the franchise network, notably with training, product development, advertising, promotional activities and with a specialist range of management services.

To further understand the franchising scenario you should do the following:

☐ Speak to current franchisees.

☐ Visit a franchise exhibition – there are major annual franchise exhibitions in Birmingham, London, Manchester and Dublin.

☐ Read the trade and national press – trade publications include *Business Franchise* (www.businessfranchise.com), *The Franchise Magazine* (www.thefranchisema-gazine. net) and *Franchise World* (www.franchiseworld.co.uk).

The BFA has an information pack which can be ordered online. It also holds regular one-day franchisee workshops at various locations across the country. At these workshops you can learn more from franchisees, franchisors, and banking and legal professionals. The course will enable you to assess whether franchising is right for you. Attendance costs £75 plus VAT.

Further information on these seminars is available from the Help & Advice page of the BFA website. There are also a number of interesting franchising books on the market and guides from the BFA, as well as the Franchise Survey which provides a detailed in-depth analysis of franchising in the UK.

Ensure the franchisor provides the following particulars:

☐ The locations being offered.

☐ Details of competitors.

☐ Details about themselves, their history and their success rates.

☐ Info on the type of support and training.

☐ All the costs involved, including the up-front fee and royalties.

☐ The projected financial returns.

☐ The terms of the agreement.

Take professional advice from a bank, a solicitor, or an accountant. Make sure that when you do so they illustrate an understanding of franchising with a BFA Affiliate membership.

RAISING FINANCE TO BUY A FRANCHISE

According to Mark Scott, National Franchise Manager at NatWest, raising finance for a franchise is not as daunting as it may seem. Most of the main banks have a dedicated franchise section only too willing to provide finance for the purchase of a franchise, although it should be noted that it will be you as an individual that they will assess, rather than the franchise.

People generally will be able to borrow more to establish a franchised business than they could for a conventional start-up venture. All the banks recognise that franchising is usually a safer way to get into business and, for established and proven franchise systems, they are prepared to lend, subject to status, up to 70% of the start-up costs including working capital. For a new or less established franchise this figure is nearer 50%, much the same as a conventional business.

Typically this borrowing will be taken as a fixed rate loan repayable over a term no longer than that of the franchise agreement. Variable rate loans are also available if you want to gamble on interest rates. Some of the borrowing could also be taken as an overdraft to provide an element of working capital. Certainly the VAT element of any franchise fee is normally funded by way of overdraft until it is refunded by HMRC.

Types of lending are normally arranged at local Business Centres and security for any borrowing may be required. Security is usually provided in the form of a second mortgage over property but could also include a charge over surplus cash, insurance policies or stocks and shares. If there is no security available the bank can look for a guarantee (up to 75% of the amount borrowed) from the government's Small Firms Loan Guarantee scheme. The remainder is considered as unsecured borrowing. The rates on any lending can vary depending on the contribution, security and track record of each individual.

Once again, your business plan is an important document.

As Mark Scott notes:

❛ It provides a guide to whether your business is going well or under-achieving. It is essential that, once written, reference is made to it from time to time to ensure any falling trends are adjusted as soon as possible and with the assistance of the franchisor. The franchisor should be interested in the performance compared to the plan, as their income should depend on the success of your business. ❜

Before any bank is willing to lend you money, a business plan will be required. Include the following in your plan:

☐ Details about the franchise.

☐ A description of the sector it operates in.

☐ An outline of the competition, both locally, regionally and nationally.

☐ Your marketing plan.

☐ The costs.

☐ The projected financial information.

☐ Your CV.

☐ Your assets and liabilities.

One of the most important sections of the plan is the details about the franchisee. The bank would want to examine the past financial performance, and accounts from the last three years would be expected.

Many franchisors will assist you in completing a business plan. However, the bank will expect you to know and understand the various statements and financial figures it contains and will undoubtedly ask questions about parts of your plan.

In the long run, the financial information you've put together, particularly the forecasts, will help you assess the performance of your deli franchise in the early months. Talk, for instance, to the NatWest Franchise section about the financial aspects of running a franchise and ask them to put you in touch with your nearest franchise manager.

OPPORTUNITIES

Franchise opportunities are available through Berits & Brown. Each shop offers three revenue streams: a delicatessen, fine wine and a coffee shop. They will find the shop premises, assist you in gaining all the licences and approvals you require, provide training, and set up your initial suppliers and Electronic Point of Sale (EPOS) system. For more information, contact Sue Berits or Peter Brown (Tel 0845-157 7527; email enquiries@beritsandbrown-franchise.com; www.beritsandbrown-franchise.com).

Other possibilities exist through:

☐ Deli Plus, 1 Tudor House, Coychurch Road, Bridgend, Mid Glamorgan CF35 5NS (Tel 01656-669400; email freshfood@deliplus.co.uk; www.deliplus.-co.uk).

☐ Franchise UK, Unit 67, Station Road, Hailsham, East Sussex BN27 2ET (Tel 0800-019 9662; www.franchise-uk.co.uk).

☐ Select your Franchise, Fryern House, 125 Winchester Road, Chandlers Ford, Hampshire SO53 2DR (Tel 0870-760 1199; email md@selectyourfranchise.-com; www.selectyourfranchise.com/uk).

☐ whichfranchise.com, 375 West George Street, Glasgow G2 4LW (Tel 0141-204 0050; email enquiry@whichfranchise.com; www.whichfranchise.com).

Further advice and information can be obtained from the British Franchise Association (BFA) at www.thebfa.org; and Franchise Development Services (FDS) at www.fdsfranchise.com.

7

PLANNING FOR SUCCESS

IN THIS CHAPTER:

GOING LOCAL

PROVIDING ORGANIC PRODUCE

STOCKING FAIRTRADE PRODUCTS

FOLLOWING FIVE-A-DAY AND OTHER TRENDS

FOOD FROM BRITAIN

BEING AWARE OF GREEN ISSUES

LOOKING AFTER YOUR CUSTOMERS

INSIDE YOUR DELI

NUTRITIONAL LABELLING

PRICING FOR PROFIT

LOGOS AND SYMBOLS

EU PROTECTED FOOD NAMES

While consumers generally will care and worry about value for money there is equally an escalating interest in food quality, provenance, health, local and regional economies, and environmental impact. In other words, people shop with one eye on the price and the other fixed on feel-good factors. For the first time in the history of the human race we are globally trying to lessen our impact on Mother Earth. One effect of this trend is to polarise the retail food market between the premium and discount ends of the spectrum.

According to the Institute of Grocery Distribution (IGD), the exact nature of the UK premium sector is hard to define, since consumers, suppliers and retailers all have their own interpretation of what defines 'premium'. The IGD defines the premium sector as one which includes products and brands which appeal to consumers on aspirational, ethical and quality grounds, such as organic, Fairtrade, locally and regionally sourced products, specialist and fine foods, and premium branded products.

Based on this definition, the IGD estimates the value of the UK premium sector to be worth at least £9.8 billion and possibly as much as £11.6 billion once an estimated value for premium branded products has been included. This represents approximately 9.6% of the UK's grocery sector. The IGD is also predicting that the value of the premium market will rise to nearly £20 billion within the next few years.

Premium products are most often viewed by consumers as those which are 'out of the ordinary', with the quality of ingredients being the key indicator of the premium standing of a product. Increasingly, values such as organic and free-range have now become closely associated with the notion of premium in the minds of consumers.

The UK's premium retail sector is currently dominated by four key retailers: Waitrose, Booths, Marks and Spencer and Sainsbury. Other retailers are continuing to develop their premium private label ranges. Tesco's Finest brand is currently worth £1 billion a year; Sainsbury's Taste the Difference range now extends to 1,000 lines; Asda is relaunching its Extra Special range, while Morrison's is expanding its The Best range. Discounters are also getting involved, with Aldi most notably introducing its own premium brand.

> *Premium market values*
>
> Organic: £1,600 million (Soil Association)
> Fairtrade: £195 million (Fairtrade organisation)
> Locally and regionally sourced products: £3,970 million (Defra/ADAS)Specialist/fine foods: £211 million (The Guild of Fine Food)
> Premium branded products: £1,854 million (IGD estimate)

IGD research shows that many retailers are enhancing their premium label range as a way of differentiating their offers in order to engage with their increasingly discriminating customers. Shoppers, while price conscious, are willing to pay the extra for something special as this helps to authenticate their own feelings both of success and their urge to do the right thing.

The average shopper equates premium with quality and as such there are high expectations that come with a premium offer. Description and product delivery need to meet such expectations. Customer service in-store is the number one factor in defining premium retailers. Shoppers are expecting to enjoy the shopping trip and quality needs to be present in every factor, from customer service, product choice and appearance, to in-store theatre, (such as customer tastings).

The IGD believes that the 'premiumisation' of the goods and grocery market represents a major opportunity for the industry and, therefore, the delicatessen business.

There is also a movement in the USA known as the Locavores: people who eat, wherever possible, food that comes from within a 100-mile radius, from farmers' markets, allotments and small shops that prioritise local producers. Locavores have a mantra: 'If not locally produced, then organic. If not organic, then family farm. If not family farm, then local business. If not local business, then Fair Trade.'

Going local

Delis selling local produce with a regional flavour, and those with trade links to local and regional producers, are becoming increasingly popular. The economic importance of local and regional food is that smaller producers can develop quality products which can be marketed locally. It is an area of economic activity with an enormous growth potential that is only just beginning to blossom.

Defra defines regional food as food produced within a geographical area, marketed from that area and sold either in or outside the area. In addition, it should have a distinctive quality because of the area it comes from or the method of production used.

According to a recent survey by The Guild of Fine Food, fine food retailers are generally closer to their suppliers and will obtain many of their products locally. British-produced goods account for more than two-thirds of the products sold. Eighty-three per cent of respondents buy direct from local producers and 55% direct from national producers, supporting the public perception of the fine food sector as both a champion and a source of products with a known provenance.

Says Gary Williamson, of Corner on the Square deli in Inverness:

Having owned and operated greengrocer stores, I knew there was a demand for local food and food with provenance. Unfortunately, the low value of fruit and veg meant that this range was not enough to support a store, so I opened a deli.

The IGD survey also found that many respondents felt that regional food groups made the biggest contribution in areas such as improving customer confidence, involving themselves with product promotion, achieving media coverage, running shows, maintaining award schemes and training. There are many groups and agencies devoted to increasing the amount of food produced and consumed regionally. Some of these are:

☐ Tastes of Anglia, covering Bedfordshire, Cambridgeshire, Essex, Hertfordshire, Norfolk and Suffolk (Tel 01473-785883; email enquiries@tasteofanglia.com; www.tasteof anglia.com). Says Sam Young, of Tastes of Anglia: 'We are dedicated to providing services to all producers, processors and purveyors of fine food and drink from the regions of our six counties. We have a distribution company, TOA Table, which delivers member products to shops and restaurants in the region. We supply mainly premium chutneys, biscuits and so on to delis.'

☐ South East Food Group Partnership, covering the Thames Valley, Hampshire and the Isle of Wight (Tel 01730-893724; email info@sefgp.co.uk; www.sourcelocalfood.co.uk).

☐ A Taste of Sussex (Tel 0845-678 8867; email info@sussexenterprise.co.uk; www.atasteof sussex.co.uk).

☐ Produced in Kent (Tel 01732-853170; email info@producedinkent.co.uk; www.produced inkent.co.uk). Says Jill Sargent, of Produced in Kent: 'We market and promote a wide range of members involved in local food and drink. We have helped many independent retailers with sourcing local products; everything from jams and chutneys to cheeses and meats to the more unusual such as fruit heather and goat's milk. We can help delis looking for local suppliers and promote their business when they become a member. Our advice is go local – great local products should be the basis of any deli worth visiting.'

☐ Buckinghamshire & Milton Keynes Food Group (Tel 01296-383345; email bucksandmk@ local-food.net; www.local-food.net).

☐ Berkshire Food Group (Tel 01635-523857; email berkshire@local-food.net; www.local-food.net).

☐ Oxfordshire Food Group (Tel 01865-484116; email oxfordshire@local-food.net; www.local -food.net).

☐ Hampshire Fare (Tel 01962-845999; email hampshire.fare@hants.gov.uk; www.hampshire fare.co.uk). Notes Susie Carter, of Hampshire Fare: 'We suggest that anyone looking to start up their own delicatessen should get in touch with their local food group as they will be a fountain of knowledge on producers in the region. Stocking the best produce from all over the world is key for a deli, but just as important is showing your customers that you actively support local farmers and that their money will go back into the surrounding countryside. A lot of food groups produce a directory of producers, which Hampshire delicatessens says is their bible when looking for new suppliers.'

☐ Island 2000 Trust, covering the Isle of Wight (Tel 01983-298098; email enquiries@island2000.org.uk; www.island2000.org.uk).

☐ Taste of the West, covering Cornwall, Devon, Dorset, Gloucestershire, Somerset and Wiltshire (Tel 01392-440745; email enquiries@tasteofthewest.-co.uk; www.tasteofthewest. co.uk).

☐ Heart of England Fine Foods, covering Herefordshire, Shropshire, Stafford-shire, Warwickshire, West Midlands and Worcestershire (Tel 01746-785185; email admin@ heff.co.uk; www.heff.co.uk). Says Claudia Baker, of Heart of England: 'We work with producers and retailers to make sourcing regional food and drink as easy as possible and can arrange meetings for suppliers and buyers. We consider the source of the products to be high on the agenda of consumer interest – food miles, carbon footprint, traceability – and therefore this should be an important point for deli openers to consider. Our delivery service provides retail outlets with regional food and drink delivered with one invoice and one delivery. This scheme not only reduces food miles but hopefully cuts down on paperwork and time for retailers.'

☐ East Midlands Fine Foods, covering Lincolnshire, Leicestershire, Nottingham-shire, Derbyshire, Northamptonshire and Rutland (Tel 0115-875 8884; email enquiries@eastmid landsfinefoods.co.uk; www.foodcampus.com).

☐ North West Fine Foods, covering Cheshire, Cumbria, Greater Manchester, Lancashire and Merseyside (Tel 01695-732734; email office@nwff.co.uk; www.nwff.co.uk).

☐ Northumbria Larder, covering Northumberland, Tyne & Wear, County Durham and Cleveland (Tel 0845-456 2340; email enquiries@northumbria-larder.co.uk; www.northumb ria-larder.co.uk).

☐ The Regional Food Group for Yorkshire & Humber (RFGYH) (Tel 01937-830354; email team@rfgyh.co.uk; www.rfygh.co.uk). Laura Gill, of RFGYH says: 'We facilitate the meeting of producers and suppliers and offer all sorts of other assistance to local food-related businesses.'

☐ Northern Ireland Food and Drink Association (Tel 02890-241010; email mbell@nifda. co.uk; www.nifda.co.uk).

SALSA (Safe Local Supplier Approval), c/o Bloxham Mill, Barford Road, Bloxham, Banbury, Oxfordshire OX15 4FF (Tel 01295-724248; email info@salsafood.co.uk; www.salsafood.co.uk) is a not-for-profit approval scheme that helps local and regional food and drink producers to meet the standards which buyers demand. Registering with them means you will be able to buy local products from suppliers who meet product safety and quality assurance standards. This is endorsed by both Defra and the Food Standards Agency.

The East of England Development Agency (EEDA) is funding work to grow the regional food sector. The aim is to help businesses, however small scale their operation, to access profitable markets and expand their operations.

A range of initiatives is also being undertaken, including a PR campaign to increase the East of England's profile as a source of quality food and drink, co-ordinating the different regional food promotions and activities and running a business trade show to promote the use of regional foods within the hospitality, food and retail sectors.

Sourcing locally means buying seasonal foods and to find out what's in season see www.bbc.co.uk/food/in_season

For local farmers' markets and places to select your own supplies, see www.farmersmarkets.net

For local farm shops there is a good interactive map at www.farmshopping.net/farm-shops.htm. All listings are inspected by the National Farmers' Retail and Markets Association at www.farma.org.uk

They can also help you via www.farmshopping.net to find suppliers of locally produced fruits, vegetables, meats, cheeses and other foods such as single-variety apple juices. Fresh produce can be picked to order and you will be able to publicise the farm from which your main ingredients came. Their website contains details of more than 450 farms and 200 farmers' markets. They also have a database of a further 1,000 farms producing foods that are sold direct to the public. If you do not find what you need on their website, call 0845-458 8420 and they will be pleased to help.

Here are a few other helpful sources:

☐ For a list of producers within easy reach of your postcode area plus mail-order specialists who deliver throughout the UK, see www.bigbarn.co.uk or www.thefoody. com

- For a list of cheesemongers and makers across the country telephone 020-7253 2114 (email info@specialistcheesemakers.co.uk, www.specialistcheesemakers.-co.uk).

- For advice on sourcing game telephone Game-to-Eat on 01273-834716 (email info@gametoeat.co.uk, www.gametoeat.co.uk).

- For details of the best sausage shops and suppliers in the UK, you can email info@sausagefans.com or check out www.sausagefans.com

- For advice on including meat from rare breeds on your menu telephone Traditional Breeds Meat Marketing Co Ltd on 01285-869666 (email info@tbmm.co.uk, www.tbmm.co.uk).

- For a comprehensive list of mutton suppliers in your area telephone The Mutton Renaissance on 0870-242 3219 (email info@muttonrenaissance.org.uk, www.muttonrenaiss ance.org.uk).

- For information on sourcing local beers and ciders telephone the Campaign for Real Ale (CAMRA) on 01727-798434 (email camra@camra.org.uk, www.camra.org.uk).

- For details of English wines, vineyards and producers, telephone 01536-772264 (email julia@englishwineproducers.com, www.englishwineproducers.com).

Providing organic produce

Eating healthier foods has become a prime topic, both for government and health organisations attempting to tackle the nationwide obesity crisis. A Euromonitor report, for instance, stated that organic foods, while once a useful niche market for delicatessens, have now become mainstream and thus command more prominent shelf space. This interest in organic produce naturally offers good opportunities for delis. Recent research by the Soil Association has put the UK's annual organic sales at £1.6 billion – and this figure is rising by at least 30% a year. The report also says that organic sales through independent outlets have increased by 32%, while a separate Soil Association report found 52% of customers who buy organic also prefer to buy from small local suppliers.

To look for organic products, go to The Organic Directory at www.whyorganic.org where you can search by region or product. The directory is also available in hard copy book form from the Soil Association (Tel 0117-914 2400; email ff@soilassociation.org; or through their online shop at www.soilassociation.org). This lists more than 2,000 retailers, producers, wholesalers and manufacturers and costs

£8.95 plus postage and packing. You can also check out the Soil Association's certification for a list of licensees in your particular area.

Stocking Fairtrade products

Ethical products that help farmers and producers in developing countries have seen an increase in recent years. Certified products in the UK have grown by 50% a year, with Fairtrade coffee accounting for more than 18% of the total roast and ground coffee market. You could meet this demand by stocking a range of Fairtrade products, such as coffee, tea, cocoa, honey, wine, dried fruits, nuts, sugar, fresh fruit and juices. Fairtrade guarantees a fair deal for disadvantaged producers and farmers by making sure they receive a fair price for their work and goods. Fairtrade items are generally slightly more expensive than similar products – but more and more people are happy to pay a little extra to help producers become self-sufficient. All Fairtrade products are marked with the easy to recognise Fairtrade mark.

Fairtrade certifies Third World farmers' produce and pays them a set minimum price for their goods, which is enough to cover their production costs and give them a living wage. In return, Fairtrade producers must meet certain standards. For most products, including coffee, cocoa, tea and bananas, the standards set a Fairtrade minimum price that covers the costs of sustainable production. These are set by the Fairtrade Labelling Organisation (FLO) International. Only those licensees, such as importers and manufacturers, who are registered with the Fairtrade Foundation can apply the Fairtrade mark to a product.

You'll probably buy your Fairtrade goods either direct from the manufacturers or importers or from registered wholesalers in the UK. The Fairtrade Foundation website has a list of wholesalers that sell Fairtrade marked products to retailers in the UK. When you buy Fairtrade goods from a wholesaler or registered manufacturer, you should expect to pay a little more than you normally would for similar products.

Although Fairtrade prices are higher, you can probably charge your customers a little bit more for them without rocking the boat. The Fairtrade Foundation isn't involved in setting retail prices, so your mark-up is entirely up to you. Offering Fairtrade products can be an appealing selling point for your deli and can help to attract ethically aware customers. The Fairtrade Foundation will also provide useful materials and advice to help you to advertise your Fairtrade ranges. Any promotional materials that contain the Fairtrade mark, like posters or leaflets, must be approved by the Foundation. Their *Manual for Promotional Materials* contains the full guidance on how the Fairtrade mark should be used. You can download this from the Fairtrade Foundation at www.fairtrade.org.uk. The Fairtrade Foundation also organises a Fairtrade Fortnight each year to promote the system. Around this time, you may want to hold a Fairtrade tasting evening where you could further promote your deli and its products.

In addition to Fairtrade, there are other ethical shopping schemes. These include the Rainforest Alliance certification (coffee, fruit and juices); Equitrade (Malagasy chocolate); and the Good African Coffee Company (Ugandan Rwenzori coffee). All these producers either benefit from a guaranteed minimum price or keep profits within the local community.

Following five-a-day and other trends

A Food Standards Agency (FSA) review into terms such as 'fresh', 'authentic', 'natural', 'homemade', and 'traditional' has prompted guidelines to be drawn up to instruct sellers on how to label the relevant produce. This affects large and small food retailers and you should be aware of this terminology and conform to the related guidelines.

Consumers' needs are changing all the time and it is important your deli responds to new trends and meets demands for convenience, variety, choice and products that offer health and nutritional benefits. Health is a dominant factor and fresh foods continue to take an increasing proportion of shoppers' spend. One of the key factors driving this growth has been the healthy eating agenda as consumers are being exposed to media coverage, including a range of television programmes which recommend following a healthy diet, and the government's campaign to persuade people to eat five portions of fruit and vegetables a day.

While these initiatives are likely to have provided a boost to a range of products which consumers will perceive as 'better for you', there is a close connection between health and freshness. This is particularly important if you decide on a fresh food offering, given that customers are more likely to shop for fresh foods on a regular basis, rather than as part of a larger weekly shop.

According to the American magazine *Deli Business*, the culinary concept called 'natural' is making its way into many niches of today's food market, including the deli. The consumer belief that natural foods are better is intense and growing stronger and the fact that conventional brands are entering the natural market is a testament to the high demand, and expected growth, in this segment.

This demand for healthy foods is having an increasing influence on the market for dairy products, eggs, oils and fats. There is a strong demand for functional products, such as pro-biotic drinks and yoghurts and cholesterol-reducing spreads and milk. Organic products are also buoyant and products that link to particular health trends, such as milk enriched with omega-3 oils, are all benefiting in growth and increased sales.

The UK confectionery market was valued at an estimated £4.41 billion in 2006, although growth is slowing as this sector is increasingly regarded as unhealthy. A move to more healthy options has occurred among suppliers with the appearance of sugar-free options, as well as the inclusion of additives such as vitamins. The most obvious trends in the chocolate market recently have been the moves towards darker, and more expensive, chocolate. The perceived health benefits of cocoa were a driver behind the move towards darker chocolates, which are also regarded as being of a higher quality. The market for condiments and sauces has equally seen only slow growth (a mere 1%) in an overall market valued at around £687 million. This slow growth is attributed to consumers moving away from barbecue and other thick sauces. Improved sales of mayonnaises and tomato ketchup have, however, made significant contributions. This has been partly due to the introduction of squeezable formats in plastic bottles, as opposed to traditional glass.

Both carbonated and concentrated soft drinks have lost market share to fruit juices, fruit-based drinks and bottled water due to their perceived healthier properties. The hot beverages' market is dominated by instant coffee and black leaf tea bags, yet it is the more niche and premium segments within coffee and tea which have shown growth and have managed to prevent the total hot beverages' market from undergoing a greater decline.

According to the Food and Drink Federation (FDF), the main driving forces for changes in consumer demand have been the growth in spending power and changes in demographics and lifestyles, which have fuelled the demand for convenience foods, value-added products and eating outside the home. This has meant that overall consumer expenditure on food (and drink) has continued to grow even though calorie intake has stagnated. These various changes seem to imply that markets have segmented more finely.

Says Gary Williamson, of Corner on the Square deli in Inverness:

> *I keep abreast of trends from a variety of sources but customers tell you a lot. Collectively, they watch a lot of TV and read a lot of the magazines that drive the popular food trade. Trade magazines and even news items all carry information which relates to your business.*

Recent trends here include:

☐ A continuing focus on health (obesity, functional foods, the replacement of 'unhealthy' ingredients such as trans fats).

☐ The continuing need for convenience.

☐ The continuing need for value.

☐ The continuing demand for premium and indulgence.

☐ Increasing consumer concerns about various environmental issues, enhancing growth in organic and Fairtrade products, and leading to concerns about food miles and the broader carbon footprint.

However, these mega-trends hide a variety of sub-trends and counter-trends that you must bear in mind and respond to in your deli business.

Mega trend	Sub or counter trend
Supermarkets merge to achieve greater economies of scale and more retail space.	Consumers support reintroduction of farmers' markets and e-shopping.
FDM sourcing and final products go global.	Consumers think local, want identifiable provenance for their food and drinks, and want to keep cultural and regional specialities.
Own label products dominate.	Biggest brands get bigger and speciality foods become more popular.
Obesity and health issues drive demand for 'health' foods.	Consumption of 'junk' food unaffected.
Convenience foods presented as an answer to increasing numbers of working men and women.	Total leisure time available in the population is increasing, particularly among the older age group segments.
Electronic retailing and virtual shopping malls increase.	Many consumers want more service and a personal touch.
Science provides ways to increase crop yields and feed conversion rates.	Environmental constraints and consumer demands pushing towards extensive food production and agriculture, low input farming, no scientific manipulation.
Genetic modification increases the possibility of new food products.	Consumers increasingly interested in natural and organic, but show a strong aversion to genetically modified products.

Source: Food and Drink Federation

Following is a list of food sectors which may help you when considering what to stock. You can contact the appropriate associations and/or groups linked to them for advice:

☐ **Biscuit, cake, chocolate and confectionery**
FDF's Biscuit, Cake, Chocolate and Confectionery Group
www.fdf.org.uk

☐ **Bottled water**
British Bottled Water Association
www.britishbottledwater.org

☐ **Bread and bakery snacks**
Federation of Bakers
www.bakersfederation.org.uk

☐ **Breakfast cereals**
Association of Cereal Food Manufacturers (ACFM)
www.breakfastcereal.org

☐ **Cheese**
British Cheese Board
www.britishcheese.com

☐ **Chilled food**
Chilled Food Association (CFA)
www.chilledfood.org

☐ **Cider**
UK Cider
www.ukcider.co.uk

☐ **Coffee**
British Coffee Association (BCA)
www.britishcoffeeassociation.org

☐ **Crisps and snacks**
Snack, Nut and Crisp Manufacturers' Association (SNACMA)
www.esa.org.uk

☐ **Dietetic food**
Infant and Dietetic Foods Association (IDFA)
www.idfa.org.uk

☐ **Fish and fish products**
FDF's Seafood Group
FDF's Shellfish Working Group
FDF's Fish Work Group
www.fdf.org.uk

☐ **Foodservice**
FDF's Out of Home Group
www.fdf.org.uk

☐ **Frozen food**
FDF's Frozen Food Group
www.fdf.org.uk
British Frozen Food Federation
www.bfff.co.uk

☐ **Herbal infusions**
Seasoning and Spice Associations (SSA)
www.seasoningandspice.org.uk

☐ **Herbs**
British Herb Trade Association
www.bhta.org.uk

☐ **Meat**
FDF's Meat Group
www.fdf.org.uk

☐ **Organic food**
Organics Group
www.fdf.org.uk

☐ **Potatoes**
Potato Council
www.potato.org.uk

☐ **Seasonings and spice**
Seasoning and Spice Association (SSA)
www.seasoningandspice.org.uk

☐ **Soft drinks and fruit juices**
British Soft Drinks Association
www.britishsoftdrinks.com

□ **Tea**
UK Tea Council (UKTC)
www.tea.co.uk

□ **Vegetarian and meat-free**
FDF's Vegetarian and Meat-Free Group
www.fdf.org.uk

□ **Yoghurt and chilled desserts**
FDF's Yoghurt and Chilled Dessert Group
FDF's Dessert and Cake Mixes Association (DCMA)
www.fdf.org.uk

Says Angus Ferguson, of Demijohn deli in Edinburgh and Glasgow:

I keep abreast of changing trends by reading newspapers, walking the streets, asking questions, keeping my eyes and ears open for opportunities and being prepared to compromise and change direction if necessary.

In a recent IGD Consumer Unit survey, when consumers were asked what the five most important product considerations were, the primary drivers which follow may help you decide what products to select:

Knowing all the ingredients in a product – 25%
It is a brand name I know – 19%
Knowing which country the food has come from – 10%
The price of food – 7%

Secondary drivers were:

Fat content – 25%
The price of the food – 22%
Sell-by-date – 21%
Salt content – 20%
Sugar content – 19%
If it is a brand name I know – 16%
If I am going to like the taste of the food – 12%
If it is environmentally friendly – 12%
Knowing which country the food has come from – 11%
Knowing about the standards of animal welfare – 10%
If the food is organic – 9%

To keep up to date with developments, join The Guild of Fine Food (www.finefoodworld.co.uk) which is the trade association representing the interests of the delicatessen sector. It offers a range of services to members, including a subscription to their *Fine Food Digest* magazine. The Guild also runs a fine food accreditation scheme. This provides deli members with a database of fine food and drink products which are sold only in independent outlets and are not therefore available in supermarkets. Their website also contains details of speciality and fine food fairs held in Glasgow, Harrogate and London.

Food from Britain

Sadly, Food from Britain, the body formed to support the growth of regional producers, is now being wound down by the current government. Says Cumbrian MP David Maclean:

> *There has never been a better time for British food and drink producers to be proud of their product and to want to promote it on the world market. The high welfare standards of the UK food industry coupled with a growing awareness of seasonality and traceability means there is a huge market for British produce, and we should be capitalising on this, not winding down the very body promoting it.*

To date, 36 British foods have had their character and reputation protected through the EU's Protected Food Name scheme. This compares with France, which has 161, and Italy, which boasts 155. On the British list so far, and worth stocking, are:

Arbroath smokies
Beacon Fell Traditional Lancashire cheese
Bonchester cheese
Buxton Blue cheese
Cornish clotted cream
Dorset Blue cheese
Dovedale cheese
Exmoor Blue cheese
Gloucestershire cider and perry
Hereford cider and perry
Jersey Royal potatoes
Kentish ale
Kentish strong ale
Newcastle Brown Ale
Orkney beef

Orkney lamb
Rutland bitter beer
Scotch beef
Scotch lamb
Scottish farmed salmon
Shetland lamb
Single Gloucester cheese
Stilton cheese (white and blue)
Swaledale cheese
Swaledale ewes' cheese
Teviotdale cheese
Traditional farmfresh turkey
Welsh beef
Welsh lamb
West Country farmhouse cheddar cheese
Whitstable oysters
Worcestershire cider and perry,

The Cumberland Sausage Association has sent through its registration to gain recognition for its famed regional banger. Says local farmer Austen Davies in his *View from the Trough*:

> *Cumberland sausage is one of those rustic culinary landmarks – like Melton Mowbray pork pies, Lancashire hot-pot, Cornish pasties, Wiltshire bacon and countless others – that have set a subliminal standard, recognized and appreciated by the eating public. People go looking for them because they know what they are getting.*

Products are either described as Protected Designation of Origin (PDO), which means they must be wholly produced and processed in one area; Protected Geographical Indication (PGI), which means one stage of their production must be in the defined area; and Traditional Speciality Guaranteed (TSG), which means they are traditional or have customary names and features that distinguish them from other similar products (see EU Protected Names).

Being aware of green issues

Green politics, anti-globalisation and growing concerns about global warming have all increased consumer knowledge about the distance food travels and the effects of various emissions on the environment. Our growing understanding of food miles means more of us are recognising the benefits of local food, from both environmental and nutritional points of view. Many companies are now measuring their products' footprints or adopting the appropriate labelling. Being environmentally aware can help you to identify new opportunities, as 'think green, think local' has become part of the shopping ethic.

An increasing number of consumers are looking for ways to become part of the environmental movement. A number are showing their support by patronising those retailers who are committed to improving the environment. They are being drawn to such retailers because they feel they are helping to save the environment and are also looking at manufacturers and retailers to provide packaging materials that are either biodegradable or recyclable.

Being aware of environmental laws can help you to anticipate and reduce the effect the environment is having on your business. Managing this can help you improve your performance and reduce costs. The environmental and financial benefits of saving energy go hand-in-hand. By finding ways to use less energy you can reduce your company's carbon footprint, combat climate change and lower your bills.

The Carbon Trust (www.carbontrust.co.uk) believes you can reduce your overall energy use by:

- ☐ Switching off equipment, where possible, over weekends and bank holidays.

- ☐ Keeping your heating thermostat at 19° C. Your heating costs will go up by 8% each time you increase the temperature by just one degree.

- ☐ Leaving space around radiators.

- ☐ Not heating storerooms which don't need to be kept warm.

- ☐ Not putting hot equipment near cooling vents.

- ☐ Maintaining your equipment properly.

In conjunction with this, consumers are driving more change by demanding less waste being thrown in their rubbish bins and are becoming more aware of the amount of packaging used on products. Packaging is directly affected by European and UK law and by waste regulation. You need to understand these regulations and any future changes. For more information, contact WRAP at www.wrap.org.uk

Finally, get one step ahead by being aware of the fact that we are about to be introduced to the notion of 'eco-eating' in the UK, not just for environmental but for basic economic reasons. This is according to the Economic and Social Research Council (ESRC), which is currently undertaking a joint study to find some answers to the complex trade-off between the environmental cost and nutritional value of different methods of food production. Eco-eating may mean eating less meat and dairy produce because of prohibitively high prices, policies limiting access to such foods because they are bad for us, and growing pressure on agricultural land making this type of food less available.

Looking after your customers

Customer service must be the number one goal in any long-term business relationship. Word-of-mouth recommendations made by satisfied customers are a powerful form of promotion and you should aim to provide a level of service that will help to bring this about. If you put your efforts into keeping your customers content, they will remain loyal to your business.

Happy customers will not only tell friends and colleagues about you, they will also be able to tell you what your competitors are doing. Offer these customers a reward for recommending your business to others. Customer loyalty schemes, such as vouchers with a discount off the next purchase, is an effective way of encouraging your existing customers to continue buying your products. Give key customers advance notice about which offers are coming up, or when you are planning something new. You should have as your motto, 'Once a customer, Always a customer.'

Ensure that popular products are always in stock and every enquiry is dealt with immediately. Keep your customers informed and ask them for feedback – and listen to what they say. If there is going to be a problem, let your customers know straight away. If a customer complains, treat it seriously and deal with it efficiently and learn from them. There may be areas of your business that you need to improve. Leave that customer satisfied with the outcome. If you are polite and handle the complaint well, you may even convert the complainant into a regular customer.

Personal service is always appreciated: addressing your customers by name when they come in and treating them as individuals can make all the difference. Exceed your customers' expectations and continually think of ways to build and improve goodwill between yourself and them.

Delivering a high level of customer service also depends on holding on to good staff. According to the online forum Talking Retail, if you care for your employees, they in turn will care for your customers. One way of improving staff retention, customer service, store standards and business efficiency is through staff training.

Staff on the front line of your business should also be trained in the right personal and communication skills. Customer care relies on the spoken skills of your sales staff.

Without it your store can never be truly customer-friendly. You staff should greet customers warmly; smile, make eye contact and look and sound cheerful; be polite, friendly and speak clearly; show a personal interest; and be helpful.

When offering product advice, think about a customer's needs. Make sure your appearance and that of the shop create the right impression. Use reliable suppliers to make sure you have adequate stock levels. If you are out of stock of a particular product, offer to order it for the customer, and keep your promise of a delivery date. If there is a delay, inform the customer as soon as possible. It may be a good idea to reward your staff for excellent customer service; they will feel more valued and in turn keener to make that extra effort.

Says Gary Williamson, of Corner on the Square deli in Inverness:

> *I am fortunate in that I had a career in the food industry and had a lot to draw on. However, this is not hugely important as long as you are prepared to learn – fast! From the day you first open, your customers will be asking reaching questions. For me it was important not to waffle but admit what I didn't know and offer to find out. Listen to your customers and be prepared for change at all times.*

Inside your deli

Everything about food is emotionally charged. Shopping for food in your deli should be visually stimulating, positive and satisfying: an upscale gourmet market experience. Generally, consumers have become quite interested in new and different food experiences, so look for ways to spice up their lives and have an enjoyable shopping experience. It's also important that you project the right image to your discerning customer base.

Merchandising visuals, rich aromatics and tasting options will favourably impact on your bottom line. Make sure your window displays are exciting and that you change them regularly. Products should be displayed from floor to ceiling to make the experience inviting and entertaining. Make passers-by drool with hunger. Tastings are also essential in that they lead to purchasing decisions. Customers who sample products that are new to them are more likely to purchase. Be on hand to explain the product further and you should have every likelihood of a sale. Cheeses that offer affordable luxury and a story that explains the origin and history of a natural product are always popular. Indeed the leading product for most delis is cheese which will account for about 25% of your turnover. Baked goods will make up around 12% and charcuterie about 11%.

The Guild of Fine Food's recent survey (see the graph below) found that virtually all their respondents used point-of-sale (POS) materials and merchandising to drive sales. Counter displays were also found useful, followed by leaflets and flyers, posters, shelf talkers and window graphics. In addition to having them in-store, you could also circulate leaflets and price lists to local businesses and issue a monthly or quarterly newsletter. All this could include product information, new lines, information about suppliers, green issues and cultural news that may affect the supply of certain foods.

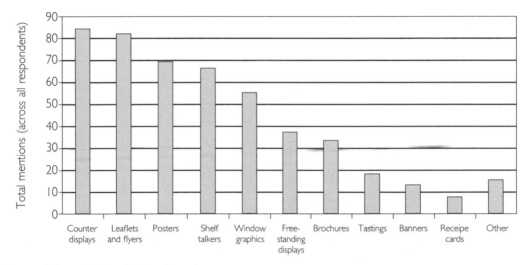

Source: The Guild of Fine Food

Says Fi Buchanan, of Heart Buchanan Fine Food & Wine in Glasgow:

> ❝ *Start with the ingredients, produce and packaging that inspire you and make sure your internal and external signage is fabulous. I was inspired by delis in New York, such as Dean and Delucca, Murrays, Gourmet Garage and Zabars. Some delis are modern, urban, and minimalistic with a few lines while others are more traditional, rural and wooden with tons of products. Both work equally well. Stick to your ethos and go for it.* ❞

Nutritional labelling

Food labels are a valuable source of information for consumers but sooner or later some of your health conscious customers are going to ask you to recommend, for example, low fat food lines and to explain to them the difference between products in terms of ingredients and their percentage of fat and other content. You'll naturally want to do this confidently and with certainty, so it's a good idea to give yourself a good grounding in the more important aspects. What follows is a broad outline of the fat, salt and sugar content in some foods, followed by the recently introduced 'traffic light' labelling, and nutritional information on labels.

It is important that consumers cut down on food that is high in saturated fat or trans fats or that they replace these foods with others that are high in unsaturated fat. The following are all high in saturated fat:

☐ Meat products, meat pies, sausages.

☐ Hard cheese.

☐ Butter and lard.

☐ Pastry.

☐ Cakes and biscuits.

☐ Cream, soured cream and crème fraîche.

☐ Coconut oil, coconut cream and palm oil.

Trans fats – chemically altered vegetable oils used to give processed foods a longer shelf life – have been banned in some cities in the USA, including New York, Philadelphia and Seattle, and also in the state of California. Trans fats are formed when liquid vegetable oils are turned into solid fats through the process of hydrogenation. While the use of hydrogenated vegetable oils has been reduced in the UK over the past few years, trans fats are still found in biscuits, cakes, pastry and some margarines. Foods that contain hydrogenated vegetable oil, which has to be listed on the ingredients label, may also contain trans fats. However, while trans fats do not need to be labelled separately under European law, the Food Standards Agency is currently working to change this because consumers say that is what they want.

Unsaturated fats which are found in oily fish, avocados, nuts, seeds, sunflower, rapeseed and olive oil spreads and vegetables oils are the healthy choice. Figures for the fat content can be found on food labels, but a high fat content means there is more than 20g of fat per 100g and a low fat content means 3g of fat or less per 100g. Saturated fat is also found on labels where high fat equals more than 5g saturates per 100g and low is 1.5g saturates or less per 100g. Omega 3 fatty acids are believed to be beneficial and can be found in vegetable oils such as linseed, flaxseed, walnut and rapeseed. However, these are not the same as those found in fish and may not have the same benefits.

Adults should have no more than 6g of salt a day. Generally, we eat about 9g a day on average. Three quarters of the salt we eat is found in the food we buy while the other quarter comes from sprinkling it on our food or adding a pinch or two to our cooking. The salt content can be found on the nutritional label. High salt equals more than 1.5g per 100g and low salt is 0.3g or less per 100g. Babies and children require far less salt: babies require less than 1g a day until they are six months old and no more than 1g a day from seven to 12 months; one to three years requires 2g a day; four to six years 3g; seven to ten years 5g; and age 11 and over 6g.

Sweets, cakes, biscuits, soft and fizzy drinks can contain high amounts of added sugar. The ingredients listed on labels may use various words for added sugar, such as sucrose, glucose, fructose, maltose, hydrolysed starch and other inverted sugar, such as corn syrup and honey. Sugar can also be listed under carbohydrates (of specific sugars) on some labels, but these do not tell you how much is from added sugars which is the type consumers should cut down on. A high sugar content is more than 15g per 100g, and low is 5g or less per 100g.

Food items with traffic light labels on the front of the pack will show if an item has high, medium or low amounts of fat, saturated fats, sugars and salt. In addition to this colour coding, the number of grams of fat, saturated fat, sugars and salt will also be included in what the manufacturer suggests is one serving of that food. A red light will show that the food is high in something that consumers should be trying to cut back on; an amber light means it isn't high or low in the nutrient; and green shows it's low in that nutrient.

Nutrition Information Typical values per 100g		
Energy	245kJ/58kcal	kJ is for kilojoules – another way of measuring energy kcal shows how many calories there are in 100g
Protein	4.6g	
Carbohydrate	7.2g	includes sugars and starch
of which sugars	6.5g	helps you work out whether the carbohydrates are mostly sugar or mostly starch
Fat	1.2g	saturated fat
of which saturates	0.2g	
Fibre	0.2g	
Sodium	0.2g	

Nutrition Information Typical values per 100g	
Energy	245kJ/58kcal
Protein	4.6g
Carbohydrate	7.2g
of which sugars	6.5g
Fat	1.2g
of which saturates	0.2g
Fibre	0.2g
Sodium	0.2g

Some labels may show allergy advice (an exclamation mark in circle), or whether this food is suitable for vegetarians (a V in a circle), or gluten free (wheat in a circle with a score through it). (For organic, Red Tractor and so on see 'Logos and Symbols' pp. 101–103.)

Davids and Goliaths

According to the FSB, independent businesses in the UK's towns and cities are facing a crisis that is posed by the endless proliferation of supermarkets and out-of-town retail developments. These business developments draw trade away from town centres by offering a wide range of discounted services and free and easily accessible parking.

With the increasing number of goods and services they provide, they offer consumers an 'all in one' shopping experience, which is convenient but often soulless. Supermarkets are thus making life very difficult for an increasing number of niche markets and independent retailers are now finding it increasingly hard to compete. The rapid growth of supermarkets across the country has already led to a huge reduction in the number of small independent retailers. Anecdotal evidence indicates that rents have been driven up in those areas where supermarkets have opened convenience branches on the high street.

This issue goes beyond price competition and raises concerns about a sustainable retail economy with an acceptable coexistence for all the parties concerned. Thriving town centres are central to any government's regeneration and sustainability objectives. Small and local retailers in such areas are providing niche goods that are unavailable in larger stores and are also encouraging local enterprise.

The FSB is urging government at both a local and national level to take steps to revitalise town centres. Unless small businesses are given the opportunity to compete, there is a risk that traditional high street shopping will continue to decline.

DEALING WITH CHALLENGES

Establishing a business can be a painful and challenging experience and familiar problems can often recur as your business matures and grows. Every business has growing pains.

Most businesses go in cycles, says the SBAS, whatever the general economic conditions. As existing customers drift away and markets shrink, businesses have to adapt by exploiting new opportunities and making new contacts. Even in the worst of economic situations, businesses can still do well.

Businesses of any age and stage can find themselves in difficulty. The first six to 24 months are often the most traumatic, with the highest failure rate being within this period. However, not all of these can count as failures, as most of these early closures are voluntary.

If you find you are barely making a living, are constantly short of cash and are working ridiculous hours, you need to have a good hard look at your business. The difficulty here is recognising the warning signs in time. A business is not really established until it is generating a reasonable income for its owner and is financially sound. Often these goals take a few years to achieve.

Mind your own business

Once you are up and running, you will need to record all the money coming into your business and all the money going out. One of the major factors that contributes to the failure of small businesses is a lack of financial housekeeping. You need an effective bookkeeping and accounting system not only because of the tax laws, but also because it will give you the following information whenever you need it:

- ☐ Cash position.

- ☐ Profits.

- ☐ Overheads.

- ☐ Variable costs.

- ☐ Debtors.

- ☐ Creditors.

- ☐ Amount of working capital.

- ☐ Stock levels.

Without proper books, you can't possibly hope to stay on top of your everyday business. It is important that the records you keep should be permanent and long lasting. Following are some of the books you should always consider keeping:

- ☐ A cash book – recording the business's income and expenditure. They come in both a hard copy and electronic format.

- ☐ A sales day book – showing who owes you money.

- ☐ A purchase day book – showing the money you owe.

☐ A petty cash account book – for recording all your minor spending, such as any postage costs and money spent on small office supplies.

Your accountant can also give you advice about other record-keeping tasks, such as inventories, stock records and replenishment systems. If your business grows and needs a more sophisticated system, you may come to need a computer and appropriate software. Your accountant can advise you about this.

There is a variety of accounting software on offer and some of the popular packages are:

☐ Microsoft Money Business and Personal: performs all day-to-day accounting functions, as well as generating up-to-date tax positions and quarterly reports. Costs about £50, including VAT.

☐ Mind Your Own Business (MYOB): offers software designed for small businesses. First Accounts is a package for start-ups and the self-employed, while MYOB Accounting is more fully featured. Costs from £199, excluding VAT.

☐ QuickBooks: offers all day-to-day functions, along with customisable invoicing and supplier tracking and an electronic invoicing and payment facility. Costs from £50, including VAT.

☐ Sage Software: offers a variety of accounting software solutions for many kinds of business. Five core packages can be augmented with additional modules to suit the individual firm's needs. Costs from £109, including VAT.

☐ Simply Books: designed as an easy-to-use package specifically for very small businesses and sole traders. It offers all the standard bookkeeping facilities as well as VAT processing and analysis. Costs from £100, including VAT.

☐ Clearlybusiness (www.clearlybusiness.com) which is a Barclays company, provides business software and subscription-based services for small businesses. Their products include:
  – Business Manager, which offers a choice between two accountancy applications, Sage Line 50 and Quickbooks Pro. It also has a human resources and health and safety service and a 24-hour legal helpline.
  – Business Essentials and Essentials Plus which features Sage or Intuit cash management software, an online training and development service, and business and marketing planning software.

Once your systems are in place, you will need to monitor your performance. You should use the information you have gathered to compare your actual figures against your projections. They will hardly ever match exactly, but if there is a significant difference, you will need to find the reason for this and decide what to do about it.

Pricing for profit

Your aim should be to set your prices at a level which gives you the highest profits possible. You need to know what customers will pay, what your competitors are charging and the costs for each of your products. There is no clear-cut or agreed way of establishing prices for your products. You could use the level of costs as a way of fixing the price but others would argue that the price should be set by what the market can bear.

It's probably best to think in terms of a range of prices. The lowest price you set should be fixed by the cost; you shouldn't go below this price. You may decide to go for prestige pricing, which means pricing your products to appeal to those of your potential customers with the highest incomes or those seeking the snob value of buying a high-priced item. Although this may mean bigger profits, it could also attract competitors offering lower prices.

Alternatively, you may want to go for backward pricing, where the customers will dictate the price they will pay. You then have to work backwards to tailor what can be provided at that price, making sure all the costs and profit margins are included. Price breaks can also be useful. For some products, it is better to break prices at 99p rather than round them up to the pound. Remember that cutting prices is not normally a good idea for any business.

According to the Small Business Advice Service (SBAS), price setting can be separated into five different stages:

Household and personal overheads per year: food, clothes, mortgage, holidays, lighting, heating, rates, telephone, tax and national insurance.

Business overheads and costs per year: your salary (household and personal overheads), rent and rates, heating and lighting, wages, advertising, stationery, interest on a bank loan or overdraft, materials, other expenses (such as legal and accounting fees).

Estimated number of sales during the period: Cost per item = $\dfrac{\text{business overheads}}{\text{estimated sales}}$

Profit you would like (say 50% of cost): Profit per item $= \dfrac{\text{Cost per item} \times 50}{100}$

The price per item, therefore = cost per item + profit.

Your gross margin therefore equals the sale price less the cost of the item. The table below shows mark-ups and gross margins on an item costing £5:

% mark-up	Sale price	Gross margin	% Gross margin
100%	£10.00	£5.00	50%
50%	£7.50	£2.50	33%
33%	£6.65	£1.65	25%
25%	£6.25	£1.25	20%

GETTING YOUR TIME AND KEY STRATEGIES RIGHT

The biggest constraint on your business is not always cash, rather your time and resources. Use your resources efficiently and effectively; it can make all the difference between success and failure. Britain's long hours culture has been well documented but you should look at ways of working smarter rather than harder. Many deli owners will create a list of tasks and prioritise them but will often not find the time for those at the bottom of the list. Identifying the important issues will make a difference to your long-term success.

According to the HSBC Bank, you also need to get your key business strategies right. Focus on your priorities by:

- ☐ Concentrating on winning and keeping customers.
  - – Continually research your customers and competitors.
  - – Work out which customers you want to target and how you will market to them.
  - – Actively promote your business and your products.
  - – Make sure you are spending enough of your time selling.
  - – Price your products competitively, but try to compete on value and service rather than on price alone.

- ☐ Monitoring your cashflow.
  - – Keep track of the balance between money coming into the business and money going out. Try to anticipate your cashflow peaks and troughs so you have time to deal with them.

- ☐ Exploring your funding options.
  - – Make sure your employees are performing effectively.
  - – Start by recruiting the right people. Use job descriptions to work out exactly what skills you want your employees to have.
  - – Lead and motivate your employees.

☐ Developing your selling skills.
  – Make sure you and your staff have the right training, aptitude and approach when interacting with customers.

☐ Controlling your costs carefully.
  – Cost control is often the easiest way to improve short-term profitability. You can possibly negotiate better deals with your suppliers.

Logos and symbols

Organic

Crops are grown without conventional insecticides and artificial fertilisers. Poultry and livestock are raised without the use of growth hormones and with only limited use of antibiotics. There are also strict welfare controls. There are a number of organic certification bodies approved by Defra but the Soil Association logo appears on about 70% of organic food produced in the UK. A new EU logo must be displayed on all organic food and drink packaging from 2009. It takes at least two years for a farmer to get organic certification. Legally a certification logo does not have to appear on packaging but it must have a certification code.

Freedom Food

Set up by the RSPCA, the Freedom Food mark indicates that the food has been approved according to their welfare standards. It applies to eggs, meat, poultry, salmon and dairy products from farm animals. It is based on the Five Freedoms and applied to each stage of an animal's life from how it is reared, fed, handled, transported and slaughtered. Regular traceability checks are carried out on the whole production process from the farm to shopfloor.

Leaf Marque

An independent scheme which stands for Linking Environment and Farming and is found on fresh and seasonal produce. While this is not organic it promotes environmentally aware and sustainable farming, whether in the UK or abroad, and is based on the holistic principles of Integrated Farm Management. It represents produce that is certified to a standard but does not represent the country of origin.

Red Tractor

Run by Assured Food Standards (AFS), the Red Tractor can be found on chicken, pork, lamb, beef, fruit, vegetables, salad, flour, sugar and dairy products. Representing everyone from farmers to retailers, it aims to raise standards in British farming, from hygiene and safety to animal welfare and the environment.

Great British Chicken

To make sure you are buying British chickens, the ASF has also come up with a Great British Chicken logo. It means that chickens and chicken products with this label can be traced back to the individual farm they came from and have been produced and packed in the UK.

Free-Range

Applies to meat, poultry and eggs. Generally, it means animals are allowed to roam free and graze as they would naturally. In the UK, the main stipulation is that a free-range chicken must have continuous daytime access to open-air runs for at least half of its life.

Quality Standard Beef and Lamb

Beef and lamb carrying the Quality Standard label will have been produced and processed through a fully assured and independently audited supply chain. The standards must relate to eating qualities such as age, sex and maturation.

Quality Standard Pork, Bacon and Ham

Products carrying these marks come from farmers and processors committed to high standards of animal welfare, quality control and traceability.

Welsh Beef and Lamb

These logos guarantee that the beef or lamb has been born and raised in Wales and has been slaughtered in an approved abattoir. These red meat products are developed, promoted and marketed through Hybu Cig Cymru – Meat Promotion Wales (HCC).

Scottish Beef and Lamb

A scheme devoted to providing quality red meat through assured standards of animal health, welfare, feeds and hygiene. The labels for Scotch Beef and Scotch Lamb can only be used for cattle or sheep that have been born, raised and slaughtered in Scotland and have been assured from birth.

Fairtrade

Covers everything from fruit, coffee and tea to spices and wine. Awarded to products that guarantee fair pay and conditions for workers in the developing world, as well as supporting smallholder co-operatives.

EU protected food names

In 1992, the European Union created a system to protect and promote traditional and regional food products. The system was devised to encourage diverse agricultural production methods, protect product names from misuse and imitation and help educate consumers. Labels have been developed to correspond to specific products requirements, as follows:

☐ Protected Designation of Origin (PDO): Products must be produced, processed and prepared in a specific region using traditional production methods. The raw materials must also be from the place indicated on the product. The quality of the characteristics of a product, such as climate, the nature of the soil and local know-how, must be due essentially or exclusively to its place of origin.

☐ Protected Geographical Indication (PGI): Requires the product to be produced in the geographical region that bears its name. The geographical link must occur in at least one stage of production, processing or preparation. It is sufficient for only one of the production stages to have taken place in the defined area, unlike PDO. This allows for a more flexible link to the region and can focus on a specific quality, reputation or other characteristic attributable to the geographical origin of the place.

☐ Traditional Speciality Guaranteed (TSG): These labels are linked to traditional production methods rather than the region. They must be produced either from traditional materials or by following traditional techniques. Any producer can use the name as long as the registered specifications are respected.

8

MARKETING YOUR DELI

Effective marketing of your deli is one of the most important factors in ensuring its success and longevity. It's all about getting your message across. Guided by your own market research, analyse how you are going to reach your target market to convey your key sales message. People can't buy from you if they don't know you exist. You must have a clear picture of your business and the benefit customers will gain from buying your products. Pricing will also be essential to your marketing programme and your location is just as important.

This makes up the marketing mix and once you have made a firm decision on product, price and place, it will lead you to the construction of your marketing and promotion plans. As mentioned in 'Researching your Market' in Chapter 2, a thorough evaluation of your competition and the anticipated strengths and weaknesses of your business will help define your market.

Says Jane Heaton, of Jane Heaton Associates, a marketing and support services company:

> ❝ *You need to move people from having no idea you even exist to being aware of what you do; to being interested in what you have to offer and telling you so; to actually experiencing a little bit of what you have to offer; to parting with cash for what you have to offer, and then buying from you again and telling their friends about you.* ❞

To draw up your marketing plan, the following ten-step approach from Wenta Business Services (www.wenta.co.uk) may help:

1. **Define your objectives**   Calculate what you need to achieve in financial terms and what you have to sell in order to get there. Set realistic, achievable targets.

2. **Take stock of your resources**   Think about the strengths and weaknesses of the business. List what equipment you have and what you need to get. Take account of any stock held. List what support will be available.

3. **Create your identity and image**   The starting point for creating a positive image is to invest in an identity – a name style and logo to appear on everything associated with your deli.

4. **Plan how to project your image**   Image and price are often linked. Reasonable prices may be seen as fantastic value for money rather than cheap and nasty. Reflect your qualities in everything you do.

5. **Profile your products**   Think of your products as a package of benefits to meet the needs of your customers. Understand the benefits of your products and what makes people buy them.

6. **Project your buying patterns**   New product launches and seasonal buying will affect sales.

7. **Analyse the market place**   How far will your customers travel, how are your competitors doing, what is the state of the market? Develop a clear understanding of the type of customer you want to target. Consider your competitors, what makes you different, and what's happening in the world that may improve or impede your deli.

8. **Timing**   Launch new products at the right time.

9. **Determine your pricing strategy**   Low prices are not always the most important buying motive and your products don't necessarily have to be cheap to attract customers. People are influenced more by their emotions than by reason.

A pricing policy will be dependent on market research, the competition, image and value for money.

10. **Design a promotional campaign** There are a number of ways to get your message across, including leaflets, email, advertising, PR, a website, and networking.

Says Sam Young, Business Development Manager at Tastes of Anglia:

> *TOA Marketing aims to assist businesses in the promotion and development of what they are doing through a range of business support packages. From a marketing point of view, I would advise potential deli owners to assess the competition in the area, including farm shops and independent retailers, and to look at the product range they are offering. A new deli should try and provide an element of difference.*
>
> *Providing local and regional options, especially on a fresh cheese or meat counter, could be a unique way of doing this. It is often good to try and build up relationships with local suppliers and involve them in the marketing process – list suppliers by a name on a counter or stick signs. By building a relationship with a supplier you can then benefit from their exposure by asking them to promote you as a place to buy the product – this works especially well with local favourites. Concentrating initially on counter offerings is then a good way to bring in the complementary products such as chutneys, jams, bread and so on. Try to promote this together so put a local cheese offering next to a local pickle offering for example.*

Grabbing their attention

Advertising and promotion are useful for building awareness of your deli. Decide on your unique selling proposition (USP): what will make customers buy from you and not your competitor? Your USP could be a better service, more convenience, easy car parking, fast delivery, delivery to the door, a wider range of products. Be careful about simply competing on price.

The three main aims of media promotion are to inform, remind and persuade your customers about your products, services and the shop itself. Make sure your target customers are reached by the media you advertise or promote yourself in. How you tell people about your business will be determined by the type of customer you aim to attract and your advertising budget.

You can also keep yourself in the public eye by advertising your deli in the local paper. Advertising is the art of telling people all about a business and what it can do for them. Your message must have enough of an impact to cut a swathe through a myriad of other advertisements and special offers. The advertising department at your local paper will be able to give you advice on cost, the area they cover and their circulation.

The aim of your advert is to increase sales and attract additional customers; to introduce a new range of products; to tell people who you are and how you plan to assist them. The food page of your local newspaper may be a useful place to advertise. Concentrate on local magazines and newspapers first; getting national exposure can be difficult. Advertising in special features, such as one that puts the spotlight on local or regional food or highlights a specific area, can be useful. It is estimated that only 30% of local newspaper readers will look beyond the headline of an advertisement so what you say must grab attention and create interest. This will then lead to a desire to visit your deli. Regional or local newspapers (85%) achieve a higher readership figure than national newspapers (67.7%).

Free newspapers and community magazines have the geographical focus needed for shops. They are, generally, cheaper per advertisement and useful for test-marketing. Trade and technical and club and society magazines may also be suitable. 'Lifestyle' or 'What's On' type magazines, especially those featuring cultural activities such as theatres, galleries and museums, would be particularly useful for promoting your deli and will appeal to your target market. Alternatively, magazines such as *Country Life* are influential because readers are passionately interested in the subject matter.

Advertising or listing your deli in the *Yellow Pages* (www.yelldirect.com) and *Thomson Local* (www.thomsonlocal.com) may be advantageous. These and other trade directories have high circulations and a long shelf life. Getting radio or TV coverage is fantastic but also difficult unless you've got something remarkable to say or publicise. In addition, articles in magazines can give the most rewarding publicity. You could consider advertising in an online directory. Joining The Guild of Fine Food will allow you to have an entry in their Deli Finder database. Membership also allows you to use the Guild's logo and be listed on its website.

Pay per click advertising has developed into an ideal solution for those business owners who have modest financial resources. Setting up internet advertising space means you can mix it with the sort of big brands that are privy to huge advertising budgets. Once you've registered with a search portal, you will be invited to enter keywords and phrases. To make the most of this form of advertising campaign, start with a small number of keywords and dedicate the majority of the budget towards phrases that will garner the most clicks.

A concise set of keywords, which accurately reflect the nature of your business, can target customers who are genuinely interested in what you have to offer. Go through your website and pick out the most relevant terms. After deciding on your key terms, the next step is to incorporate those keywords into the advert's text. When your pay per click campaign is up and running, the next step is to employ more advanced functions such as time scheduling and advert targeting. Dedicating £3 per day to search engine marketing will open up a whole new world of sales opportunities.

DIRECT MAIL

Producing a professionally designed leaflet or brochure showing samples of your products is another way to reach your target market. Include information on the countries of origin and traditional or innovative ways of using the products in cooking. A direct mail campaign can spread your message to potential customers. Even if the costs of design, print and mailing may be high, it can still be a useful tool for your business.

The only disadvantage here is that low response rates are a fact of life – 1% to 2% can be considered a success and many businesses do a lot worse than that. The balance may be closer to 50:50 but an envelope with a handwritten address to a named individual using a stamp is the most likely way for your information to be opened and read. Compile your mailing list through your existing customers, the web, directories in your library, your trade association, or the electoral role. Suppliers may also be able to suggest other prospects. Renting a mailing list may also be cost-effective; £100 to £120 per 1,000 names is normal. You can get a list of database members from the Direct Marketing Association (www.dma.org.uk) or in the *Yellow Pages* under 'direct mail'. You can also get more information from the Royal Mail (www.royalmail.co.uk).

PRESS RELEASES

As part of your marketing campaign, it is worth taking the time to prepare a press release to send to local or national newspapers, magazines, or television companies. However, you still have to grab the reader's attention immediately and ensure that they will read on. Start with a snappy title and list all the key points that make your business special. Then decide on your message or unique selling point and consistently put that across. Start with the most salient points and use simple, direct language. A quote or testimonial from a customer or supplier is always useful. Including a photo increases your chances of coverage.

Think about what the media are looking for; they will generally want a story, preferably one they haven't heard before. Find out the specific journalist's name and send your correspondence to them direct. Convince them why they should feature you. Your press releases should answer the journalist's five basic questions of: Who? What? Where? Why? How? Follow the 'style' of the publication and add your contact details. You can always contact the same journalist again with reminders of seasonal products and special days, but don't overdo this as it can work against you. You can find a list of all the national and regional papers, magazines and broadcast media at www.mediauk.com

At the end of the day, the most cost-effective promotion is by word of mouth. If satisfied customers recommend your business to friends, family and colleagues. This is the sort of advertising that money simply can't buy. Aim for this by consistently exceeding your customers' expectations; satisfying your customers with work well done; having a good relationship with your customers; building up a good reputation and protecting it by sorting out any problems quickly.

When SmallBusiness.co.uk posed the question: 'Which marketing strategy works best for your business?' to their readers, they received the following responses:

☐ Radio ads – 0%

☐ Sending email alerts – 2%

☐ Local newspaper ads – 2%

☐ Cold calling – 7%

☐ Sending direct mail – 12%

☐ Advertising online – 15%

☐ Word of mouth – 62%.

Developing a website

The internet is now a major force for businesses and is widely embraced as an excellent communications tool. The promotion of your website should be an integral part of your marketing strategy and your overall business plan. It is a vital tool for promoting your company and selling your products and services. It can also provide information for other people, whether they are suppliers, lenders, or staff.

There are three kinds of website:

☐ Simple homepage – this works as a simple communications tool.

☐ Showcase website – this works if you want a more detailed explanation of your product range.

☐ Online webstore – this works for online sales.

A simple homepage can be a starting point to keep in touch with customers and to attract new ones who are browsing the internet. It should include your name and logo; a description of your business activity; summary of your products and service; photographs of your products; your contact details and opening hours; and a request for feedback. It is suitable for aiming at local customers and is also a cost-effective option because it needs minimal maintenance.

A showcase website is the equivalent of putting your brochure online. It will contain the same information as a homepage but with more pictures of your product range or product groups (such as organic) spread over a number of pages. You need to keep this simple – don't make it difficult to load or provide navigation that is too complicated. Update it regularly with new information and products. If you pay an outside company to host your website, make sure you can update it as and when you like.

An online webstore should be developed when you are ready to do business online. You will need to fulfil customers orders from anywhere in the country within three days; deal with problems, late deliveries, refunds and exchanges; and operate secure debit and credit card payments.

Examine your business and decide what type of website you need. Consider whether you want to build and update the site yourself with an easy to set up and administer template-based service, or whether you need the help of a design agency. If you feel confident enough to build the page yourself there are many programs available, such as Microsoft FrontPage, Dreamweaver and Coffee Cup. Most packages offer templates or automated wizards to help you get started. Some providers can supply off-the-shelf packages for £200 or so, followed by a monthly fee of £20 or more to rent space for your site.

If you commission a web designer, you will need to create a detailed brief to help the designer create a website that meets your needs. You will also need to make ongoing changes to your website, such as prices. Your designer may do this for you for a fee, but it may be cheaper to buy your own copy of the software to edit the content.

Your website should be quick to download, easy to navigate, up-to-date, and logical in its organisation and structure. By law it must comply with the Disability Discrimination Act, which requires you to ensure it can be accessd by anyone with a disability. For more information, contact the Disability Rights Commision (www.drc-gb.org). You may also be affected by the Data Protection Act if you collect, store, or process personal data, and the EU Distance Selling Directive.

Choosing domain names

It is often beneficial to use your business name for your domain name (URL). If not, ensure it is a name that best represents your deli's interests. A domain name is the unique address through which every website on the internet can be recognised. These are generated from a huge variety of sources, but they all end up on a central register so that customers everywhere can find your website with the help of a search engine.

Some characteristics of successful domain names include being brief, memorable and distinctive. They can only contain letters, numbers and dashes. Don't have any hyphens and avoid confusion with another business with a similar name. Many of the more obvious names have been taken so it's worth coming up with a shortlist of acceptable names.

You can register your domain name through any number of domain name registration websites in the UK and these cost from about £3 per name per year. By typing 'domain name registration' into any search engine, you will find those that provide name registration cheaply and others who include name registration as part of an overall package, including web hosting and email. If you register more than one domain name they will all point to the same site.

Choose a reputable domain name supplier. Several websites will act as brokers. You can go on to one of these sites and browse the domain names that are for sale or put in a request for the name you want if it ever comes up for sale. Brokers include www.Pool.com, www.Sedo.co.uk, www.Snapnames.com and www.Dotpound.com. Don't divulge a name you require to anyone before registering it as this can be monitored. You can check a name through www.myrequiredname.com. When you are ready to register your name, go to www.netbenefit.uk. Nominet (www.nic.uk) is the organisation that maintains the registry of domain names in the UK. You can check the names which are unavailable and it has a good FAQ on all aspects of the naming process.

If you buy a domain name, make sure you also buy the other top level domains (TLDs) for the same prefix (for example .com or .net). This will make sure that no one else can capitalise on your brand name at a later stage. You can equally buy a domain name through an online seller, such as 1&1 (www.1and1.co.uk) or UK2Net (www.uk2net.net). Domain names that are bought must be renewed every two years. Remember, you don't own a domain name you only rent it. A lot of small firms get their fingers burnt because they forget to renew their domain name. There's a whole industry out there engaged in 'sniping'. These companies bide their time until your domain name is going to expire and the second it does they will have an automated piece of software to swoop in and buy it. Once they have done so, you have no further right to that domain name.

Web hosting

A web hosting provider will host your site on their space on the world wide web and make it available to the public. Depending on how your website was designed will determine which web host to use: if you have a FrontPage website, you'll need a web host who supports FrontPage. To find the right web host, check out the many web hosting directories on the web. These directories have been set up to allow you to search using the features that you're looking for in a web host. Decide on a few and then visit the many web hosting message boards and forums. See if your potential host is listed and what other people's experiences have been with them.

Most web hosts have multiple plans you can choose from. Contact them and make sure that they provide the features you need. The majority will require you to sign up by using a credit or debit card. Your internet service provider will probably also offer web hosting, but some of the others include:

☐ www.spanglefish.com which offers free websites (and hosting) with small Google ads on them. If you pay £25 per annum you can get rid of Google ads and end up with an impressive site.

☐ Freezone Internet (www.freezone.co.uk) which offers web hosting, design and domain names.

☐ 1-2-3-reg.co.uk which offers hosting from £1.48 a month.

Getting noticed on the web and elsewhere

Research shows that when people are searching the web hardly anyone will bother to look beyond the first page of results even when the search produces hundreds of them. So, to get your company noticed, you need to give your website name enough pointers for it to be automatically located on the first page.

Once you register your site address, the search engine will scan and index your pages every few weeks or so. This uses software called a spider to crawl over your site looking for keywords that are known as metatags or meta descriptions. These keywords are then used to create your webstore's listing.

Use a search engine, such as Google, Alta Vista, Yahoo, Lycos, or Ask.com, or do your own keyword research through www.wordtracker.com. Google has a PageRank system where all the web pages indexed by them are ranked. By getting your business into the relevant business directories and being mentioned in online articles, you will increase your link popularity and improve your rankings. Adding new contacts and refreshing your site regularly will have the same effect. Search engines tend to reward sites with high quality content.

Search engines generally provide a free service (both indexing and retrieval) but it is time consuming. It may be worth spending between £50 and £100 with a specialist agency that will register your website as effectively as possible with all the best search engines and web directories. Type 'registering my website' into a search engine to find more details. You can also utilise a web directory, such as iNeed, Yahoo or ShopSmart, which uses editors to review your site and create listings from descriptions that you will submit to the site editors.

Says John Courtney, of Strategy Consulting:

> *Some companies can charge anything from £1,000 to design and build your website but search engine optimisation is more important than the design and build, as without it customers won't find you. You should spend more on the optimisation than the design and build.*

Apart from search engine optimisation, traditional forms of marketing are still applicable to ebusiness. Your target customers may not be internet users or have any reason to expect an online service from you. A newspaper advertisement or flyer can be very effective in such cases. You can use a service like Google Adwords or Yahoo Sponsored Search where you pay for a short advert and a link to your site to appear on their search pages. You are charged on a cost per click basis, so that you only pay when someone clicks on your advertised link.

Incorporate your website on all of your printed material: advertising copy, letterheads, business cards, email signatures, even invoices. Your local press may also be interested in any seasonal products or offers. Use newsletters to advertise special promotions or seasonal produce. Your own network of contacts and customers will be the best search engine of all. Word of mouth is a great way to persuade internet shoppers to surf their way to your site.

Internet service providers

There are many ISPs in the market that cater for business customers. Before choosing, consider the number of email addresses they have for you to use; whether they can host your chosen name; the access to templates and building site tools; the shopping cart facilities; whether you can switch providers when and if you feel it is necessary; the fees involved; the contract.

Look for a high-speed internet service that offers low contention, which means fewer businesses are using the same service at the same time as you. Select a supplier and package that offers unlimited usage limits. Even if you may only occasionally need it, it is vital for business use: you don't want to reach a download limit or be charged extra for receiving a vital file.

Evaluate your own level of technical expertise, as this will have considerable bearing on how much support you will need from a supplier. Consider whether your deli depends on being connected to the internet for its day-to-day running. If so, it may be worthwhile considering a supplier that offers round-the-clock support, which should be included in the package with no hidden extra costs.

There is a general lack of clear information about internet connections. While details of broadband speeds are readily available other factors – such as the effect that 'contention ratios' (the ratio of other people sharing your connection) and the distance a user is from the exchange can have on download and upload speeds – are not always made clear by some suppliers.

Although you can access broadband services via satellite or wireless, most consumers receive their service via the existing telephone lines (DSL), or via cable (Virgin Media) where the provider will run a cable into your property from the main street cable (or your existing TV cable). Download rates will be similar to the DSL service. The most popular type of DSL in the UK is Asymmetrical DSL (ASDL).

There is a blizzard of options, but the Top 10 reported ISPs are:

PlusNet
Sky Broadband
Pipex
Tiscali UK
Virgin Media
AOL Broadband
BT Broadband
Talk Talk
Tesco
Orange

Your ISP should be able to offer reliable connection speeds, faster downloads, good customer service, and a competitive price. Consider the level of service you will get after a 12- or 18-month contract, rather than let yourself be swayed by advertising and introductory pricing offers.

Setting up your web store

Online retailing is continuing to boom in the UK in spite of pessimism about the economy, according to a survey conducted by the retail analysts Verdict Research. This growth rate, the fastest in six years, is about ten times that of the UK's retail market as a whole.

But physical shopping is far from doomed. 'There is still a need and place for physical locations – the key is to ensure that synergies with online retailing are exploited to drive footfall to the stores,' says Verdict. 'While having an internet presence is vital, giving the consumer choice by establishing strong links between the in-store and online offers is now essential.'

Taking your business online demands more than simply designing a functioning webstore. It will also need careful planning and logistical preparation. You must be able to respond to email enquiries promptly and deliver your goods on time. This will maximise the sales and the loyalty opportunities that the internet presents. Respond by using an automated email response to let your customers know you've received their enquiry. An email contact/ordering system could increase both your prospects and customers. For seasonal produce and specialities, customers will often travel outside their usual area to buy.

Another advantage is that your webstore will be open 24 hours a day, seven days a week, and it will be available to anyone, anywhere in the world. A number of software suppliers have already introduced complete ebusiness solutions packages that can generate your shopfront and supply all the supporting services including hosting and payment services.

You can get to know your customers by requesting registrations which will provide useful information, such as their email addresses, postal addresses, product preferences and so on. To overcome resistance to registration, use special offers, new product details, newsletters and competitions. Make clear your commitment to maintaining confidentiality and the non-disclosure of email addresses to third parties.

Your ordering process will need to include packaging, delivery, insurance and tax. You must set up a virtual shopping cart resulting in a simple single payment. The most popular form of payment is the credit card but processing these is quite high risk, so establish a merchant account with your bank, or use PayPal or WorldPay. Your customer's bank, your merchant account bank, your payment services provider, and the credit card network (Visa/Mastercard) are all the parties involved in a credit card purchase and each will charge a fee. Compare the charges and services from site builders, payment service providers, hosting businesses, banks and IT companies before you 'set up shop'.

Ensure your site is constantly evolving. Keep it fresh with regular updates, special offers, accurate information about your products and service, clear pricing and delivery details. This way you will drive repeat traffic. Make sure there are quick and easy steps to the checkout and emphasise your security and payment policies to reassure your customers further.

YOUR WEBSITE CHECKLIST

☐ Set out your objectives, for example, marketing to existing or potential customers, providing product and sales support, making direct sales or recruiting employees.

☐ Look at competitors' and other websites to generate ideas; develop an outline of what you want your site to include.

☐ Assess your technical requirements: for example, how large the site will be and whether it will use any special technologies, including product ordering and secure payment.

☐ If setting up a trading site obtain merchant status that allows you to accept credit card transactions; assess any legal and liability issues.

☐ Check all in-house and outsourced back-up resources: dispatch and delivery, customer support, stock control and replenishment.

☐ Confirm your internet service provider (ISP) will be suitable for hosting your site; check all costs and the process for publishing and maintaining web pages.

☐ Source any technical or web design consultancy you need; ask for references and evidence of successfully completing similar projects. Make sure that the design or copyright is assigned to you.

☐ Establish design guidelines that are in keeping with company style; aim for visual clarity and easy navigation; avoid complex graphics which are slow to download; consider developing a site which allows users to access a text-only version.

☐ Consider accessibility issues for disabled users and ensure your compliance with the Disability Discrimination Act.

☐ Register your desired domain name.

☐ Build the site; ensure that pages include appropriate keywords, meta tags and page descriptions to help search engines list them.

☐ Test the site, using different versions of various browsers, to ensure that the pages download quickly and the page links work.

☐ Assess the site's appeal and ease of navigation; ask your employees and key customers for any feedback and suggestions.

☐ Launch the site; register it with search engines to make it easy to find, and identify other sites you can link to and from.

☐ Promote the site: by emailing target customers for example, and include its address in your letterhead, brochures and advertising.

☐ Monitor the usage and how effective the site is at achieving its aims.

☐ Keep the site up to date; add new, time-critical material, particularly on the home page, to keep visitors coming back.

Using forums and networking

Informal networking, such as joining your local Chamber of Commerce or Business Link, can be very useful when working for yourself. Developing contacts and drawing on the expertise of others is paramount. You can forge alliances and obtain the know-how you may need to keep a competitive edge. Have clear objectives in mind when developing relationships as this can help to ensure they are beneficial to your business. When you go to a more formal networking event, such as a conference or trade show, arm yourself in advance with some interesting news about your business.

Says Michael Goswell of Locate East Sussex:

The importance of business networks cannot be over estimated for start-up businesses to share experiences and find out what works in the area. Chambers of Commerce can often give you a ready made network to tap into.

In conjunction with Lloyds TSB, the NFEA run a series of local 'Ask the Expert' events aimed at helping you find answers to some of the most important questions about starting your business. These are themed knowledge events where experts will each host a table and you will move between tables. Such experts may include solicitors, accountants, IR advisers, specialist advisers and so on. These events are generally aimed at 0–3 year old businesses, but may also be targeted at specific subsets such as ethnic minorities or women in business. For information on your local events, contact your local NFEA member.

The food retail trade associations and trade press should be able to let you know about other suitable networks. Some organisations will offer online networking opportunities where you can post messages for help on a specific issue.

Trade shows and food fairs

Trade shows and food fairs can also provide a direct route to customers. Make sure you pick an event which will be attended by your target customers and check with the organisers about their previous attendance statistics. The Guild of Fine Food's recent survey found that 77% of respondents cited the importance of exhibitions and trade fairs as sources of new ideas and suppliers.

According to the organisers, retailers taking part in the British Food Fortnight have increased their sales by up to 34% as a direct result of the event. Sales of British food and drink increased by up to £2,000 a store during one recent fortnight.

To capitalise on this sales opportunity, retailers are invited to run British food promotions during the event: to offer tastings and promotions to highlight new products, to encourage producers to come in-store to meet customers, and to decorate stores with suitable bunting and British Food Fortnight posters.

British Food Fortnight is a national celebration of the diverse range of food that Britain produces. The actual dates change every year but the event is always the last week of September and the first week of October. More information is available from Alexia Robinson or Jennifer Meakin (Tel 020-7840 9292; email info@britishfoodfortnight.co.uk; www.britishfoodfortnight.co.uk).

Alternatively, there is the Scottish Food Fortnight, a national promotion of Scottish food and drink. Here you can develop links with local suppliers and increase the amount of Scottish products you sell. For more information and to find out the dates of the annual event, contact Scottish Food Fortnight, Scottish Countryside Alliance Educational Trust, West Mains Cottage, Royal Highland Showground, Ingliston, Edinburgh EH28 8NF (Tel 0131-335 0200; www.scottishfood fortnight.co.uk).

The Speciality & Fine Food Fair is held in Glasgow, Harrogate and London every year. According to the organisers, it is the premier event for delicatessens and anyone involved in the food and drink industry to source the highest quality artisan food and drink. There is a plethora of fine food companies showcasing a range of locally sourced and international products. The London show is organised by fresh rm (www.freshrm.co.uk) and the Glasgow and Harrogate shows by The Guild of Fine Food (www.finefoodworld.co.uk).

The International Food & Drink Trade Exhibition (www.ife.co.uk) is dedicated to innovation and held annually at ExCel in London. There is also the BBC Good Food Show (www.bbcgoodfoodshow.com) which is held at the NEC in Birmingham. Fairtrade Fortnight (www.fairtrade.org.uk) and World Fair Trade Day (w.wftday.org) are regular events supporting ethical trading. Each involves the sort of events that may be of interest to you.

Here are some interesting visitor statistics from the recent Speciality & Fine Food Fair in Harrogate:

Region where visitors business is based
Scotland – 1.7%
North West – 19.4%
North East – 4.7%
Yorkshire/Humber – 54.5%
Anglia/East Midlands – 12.6%
West Midlands – 2%
Wales – 1.2%
London and the Home Counties – 2.4%
South West – 1.2%
International – 0.3%

Business activity
Catering – 22.5%
Retail – 50.9%
Wholesale/distribution – 6.4%
Manufacturing – 11.4%
Trade association – 1.2%
Other – 7.6%

Business type
Bakery/biscuits – 3.0%
Cafe/sandwich bar – 8.4%
Delicatessen – 24.6%
Farm shop – 10.3%
Foodhall – 2.9%
Hamper company – 1.9%
Health food/organics – 3%

Hotel – 2.3%
Independent retailer – 7.7%
Media – 0.5%
Pub/restaurant – 5.8%
Supermarket – 2.8%
Wholesale – 7.2%
Other – 19.6%

Visitors' areas of interest
Bakery – 61%
Cheese/dairy – 60%
Condiments – 53%
Confectionery – 48%
Drinks (alcoholic) – 38%
Drinks (non-alcoholic) – 42%
Fish/seafood – 30%
Hampers – 39%
Ice cream – 34%
Ingredients – 40%
International specialities – 40%
Jams/preserves – 49%
Meats/meat products – 38%
Oils/vinegars – 45%
Organics – 46%
General speciality products – 37%
Packaging and design – 38%
Pasta – 37%
Regional foods – 58%

Well-established but relative newcomer, National Independent Week campaigns to help raise awareness of local retailers and increase sales while rewarding consumers for shopping; this is focused purely on the positive values to the community provided by independent retailers. By supporting this campaign and becoming involved in your local community, you should be able to use it as a platform for increased footfall – which means more feet coming through your door.

9
UNDERSTANDING THE RULES AND REGULATIONS

IN THIS CHAPTER:

FOOD LAWS, HYGIENE AND SAFETY

HEALTH AND SAFETY

LICENCES

LABELLING

ENVIRONMENTAL DAMAGE

DISABILITY DISCRIMINATION

RULES ABOUT MENUS

The implementation of regulations, and the monitoring of new ones, together represent one of the greatest barriers to growth that you may face. According to the FSB, the administrative burdens for small business are five times more costly and take five times longer to process than for larger businesses. Successive surveys by the FSB have found that small businesses today are more dissatisfied with the complexity of regulations than with the volume and the cost of compliance. The FSB states:

> *Small businesses want to comply and operate within the law and they strongly support actions against businesses that deliberately ignore their responsibilities and refuse to comply with regulations. However, compliance is best achieved by offering help and guidance to enable them to do so. Local authorities and enforcement agencies must appreciate that non-compliance is often a result of poor information on the introduction of, or amendment to, regulation.*

The vast majority of new regulations originate from the EU or central government, but local authorities are required to interpret and enforce the majority of them. The

FSB believes that local authorities need to be sensitive to the challenges small businesses face in order to achieve their compliance within a complex and changing regulatory regime.

The current government is expected to introduce a new streamlined approach to the regulation of small business. This may mean exempting small businesses from regulation where this is not possible. Other approaches will include simple guidance and easy to use forms. The target is to reduce administrative burdens by at least 25% by 2010 and if this comes to pass it should make a difference to you if you are having to tackle complicated regulations.

According to the CBI, this simplification of regulation will include:

☐ Removing regulations from the statute book, leading to a greater liberalisation of previously regulated regimes.

☐ Bringing together different regulations into a more manageable form and restating the law more clearly.

☐ Using 'horizontal' legislation to replace a variety of sector specific 'vertical' regulations and to resolve overlapping or inconsistent regulations.

☐ Reducing administrative burdens by simplifying forms and increasing the intervals between information requests and shared data.

Food laws, hygiene and safety

The Food Standards Agency is the central government department responsible for food safety and hygiene legislation, but when you set up your deli you will also need to speak to the Environmental Health Department (EHD) in the borough, district or unitary council in which your business is located.

'The Environmental Health Officers (EHOs) will be able to give advice on hygiene and safety especially relevant to your business and are in the best position to determine which parts of food law apply to delicatessens,' says Bill Drennan of the Food Law Policy Branch of the Food Standards Authority.

You need to register with the EHD at least 28 days before opening. Contact your local authority for information on how to register. If you will be using two or more premises, you will need to register all of them. There is no charge for registering. Any business involving the preparation or sale of food is subject to a range of legislation governing labelling, safety, hygiene and traceability. The key regulations include:

□ The Food Hygiene Regulations 2006 (England, Scotland, Wales and Northern Ireland), which cover food hygiene, the registration of premises, cleanliness, the provision of equipment and facilities, temperature control and so on. This also includes Hazard Analysis Critical Control Point (HACCP) safety management, which involves documenting safe practices.

□ The Food Safety Act 1990, which includes legislation to ensure that all foodstuffs are safe to eat and the description of food is not misleading.

□ The Food Safety 1990 (Amendment) Regulations 2004 and the General Food Regulations 2004, which means all food businesses must establish a system whereby products can be traced back to the supplier concerned. This means recording the name and address of the supplier, the nature of the products, and the delivery date.

□ The Food Labelling Regulations 1996, which outlines labelling requirements for most foods before delivery to the consumer, and apply to the packing and promotion of foods for human consumption.

□ The Food Labelling (Amendment) Regulations 2004, which brought the UK into line with a European Union Directive to inform consumers about possible allergens contained in food.

□ The Plastic Materials and Articles in Contact with Food Regulations 1998, which implemented European directives relating to plastic materials and articles intended to come into contact with food. The Materials and Articles in Contact with Food Regulations 2005 set out further technical requirements for food packaging.

□ The Weights and Measures Act 1985, which covers the requirements regarding units and standards of measurement.

If you are going to employ staff, you should be aware of the Health and Safety at Work Act 1974, which requires you to provide the necessary information, training and supervision to ensure your employees' health and safety.

Delicatessens are also affected by trading laws, including the Sale of Goods Act 1979, the Supply of Goods and Services Act 1982, the Consumer Protection Act 1987 and the Trade Descriptions Act 1968.

If you intend to trade online, you must be aware of the Consumer Protection (Distance Selling) (Amendment) Regulations 2005, which apply to contracts for goods or services purchased by a consumer where the contract is made exclusively by means of distance communication, either through mail order or internet sales. They outline both parties' rights to cancel a contract.

FOOD SAFETY

The main safety risks are food poisoning and food allergies. Make sure you have a good knowledge of both; food allergies can be potentially life threatening.

The FSA has produced simple guidance about food safety management: *Safer Food Better Business.* 'The pack for retailers may be the most relevant, but we would suggest that those planning to start a delicatessen business consult with their local environmental health departments to make sure,' says Bill Drennan.

Your premises will need to be kept clean and maintained in good repair and condition. They must allow for you to follow good food hygiene practices, including protection against contamination and, in particular, pest control.

You must put in place 'food safety management procedures' based on the principles of HACCP. You need to keep these in place permanently; keep up-to-date documents and records relating to your procedures and remember to review these if you change what you produce or how you work. The regulations are designed to be flexible so they are in proportion to the size of your business.

A hazard means something that could be dangerous which means your food will not be safe to eat. This could be microbiological (when certain foods are kept out of the fridge for too long and bacteria grows) or chemical (cleaning products or pest control chemicals getting into food). These hazards can happen at any stage – from taking deliveries to serving customers.

The following rules must apply to your whole premises, not just the areas used for preparing food:

- □ **Handwashing facilities and toilets** You must have enough washbasins for your staff to wash their hands, with hot and cold running water and materials for cleaning hands and drying them hygienically. Separate sinks must be provided, where necessary, for washing food and cleaning equipment. There must also be enough toilets and these must not lead directly into areas where food is prepared or kept.

- □ **Changing facilities** You must provide adequate facilities for staff to change their clothes where necessary.

- □ **Other requirements** Your premises must also have adequate ventilation, lighting and drainage.

Food preparation areas

If you intend preparing food, the following rules must apply:

- **Floors and walls**   Must be maintained in a 'sound condition.' They must be easy to clean and, where necessary, disinfected.

- **Ceilings**   Must be constructed and finished in a way that prevents dirt from building up and reduces condensation, mould and the shedding of particles. In practice, this means that ceilings should be in good condition, smooth and easy to clean, with no flaking paint or plaster.

- **Windows**   Windows and any other openings must be constructed in a way that prevents dirt building up. Windows and any other openings (such as doors) that can be opened to the outside must be fitted, where necessary, with insect-proof screens that can be removed easily for cleaning.

- **Doors**   Must be easy to clean and, where necessary, to disinfect.

- **Surfaces:** Surfaces (including the surfaces of equipment) in areas where food is handled, particularly those that are touched by food, must be maintained in a sound condition and be easy to clean and, where necessary, to disinfect.

- **Facilities for cleaning equipment**   Your premises must have adequate facilities, where necessary, for cleaning, disinfecting and storing utensils and equipment. The facilities must have an adequate supply of hot and cold water.

- **Facilities for washing food**   You must have adequate facilities for washing food. Every sink (or other facilities) for washing food must have an adequate supply of hot and/or cold water. The water must be of drinking quality. These facilities must be kept clean and disinfected.

- **Equipment**   All items, fittings and equipment that food touches must be kept in good order, repair and condition in a way that enables them to be kept clean and to be disinfected. All must be effectively cleaned and disinfected frequently enough to avoid any risk of contamination.

- **Waste**   You must remove food waste and other rubbish from rooms containing food as quickly as possible, to avoid it building up. You must also have adequate facilities for storing and disposing of food waste and other rubbish.

Staff and food protection

You must make sure that any member of staff who handles food is supervised and instructed and/or trained in food hygiene in a way that is appropriate for the work they do. They must maintain a high level of personal cleanliness and wear suitable, clean clothing.

The person (or people) responsible for developing and maintaining your business's food safety management procedures, based on HACCP, must have received adequate training to enable them to do this. There is no legal requirement to attend a formal training course or attain a qualification, although many businesses may want their staff to do so.

The necessary skills could also be obtained in other ways, perhaps via on-the-job training, self-study or relevant prior experience. It is a good idea to keep a record of any training that you or your staff have undertaken, because then you will be able to show this to enforcement officers when they visit your premises.

Suppliers and food preparation

Your choice of supplier is important because of the safety and quality of the food they supply and their own reliability could affect your business. It is especially important that the products you purchase have been stored, processed and handled safely.

When food is delivered, check the following:

☐ That chilled and frozen food is cold enough.

☐ That packaging is not damaged.

☐ That it is what you ordered.

If you do not think the food a supplier has delivered has been handled safely, reject the delivery, if possible, and contact your supplier immediately.

Traceability

You must keep written records of all the suppliers that provide you with food or any food ingredients. The records should include the name and address of the supplier, the type and quantity of products and the dates on which you ordered and took delivery. You may also wish to record the batch number or the use-by or best-before date. Often this information will be on the invoice, but you should make sure of this.

You should keep all the invoices and receipts for any food products you buy from any supplier, including from a shop or cash-and-carry. This is worth doing so that if there is a safety problem with food you have sold, you or your enforcement officer can check the details of the food. Bear in mind that if food has a long shelf-life, you will need to keep your records for longer.

If you supply food to another business, you also need to keep records containing the same details. Make sure that you keep all your records in a way that means you can quickly find the details of a particular food when asked to do so by an enforcement officer.

Product withdrawal and recall

If you have supplied some food to another business and you find out that it is harmful to health or unfit for people to eat, you will need to arrange for it to be withdrawn from sale. Where it may have reached consumers, you will need to arrange for its recall, which means the consumers must be asked to return or throw away the product, unless there is another way of protecting them – ask you local authority for advice. If you withdraw or recall any food, then you must also tell the environmental health service at your local authority and the Food Standards Agency.

Transport

If you transport food – to your premises or to another venue, or from the cash-and-carry to your premises – you must prevent it from becoming contaminated, for example with dirt or bacteria.

It is especially important to make sure of the following:

- ☐ That food is transported in packaging or containers that protect it from contamination.

- ☐ That chilled and frozen foods are kept at the right temperature (some businesses use cool bags and boxes, or refrigerated vans).

- ☐ That raw and ready-to-eat foods are kept apart.

- ☐ That any vehicles used to transport food must be kept clean and in good repair.

Health officers can take enforcement action to protect the public. This includes taking samples of food; inspecting your records; asking you in writing to correct any problems; serving a formal legal notice setting out what you need to do and forbidding you from using certain premises and equipment; and, finally, recommending that you should be prosecuted if it is a serious case.

The four main things to remember for good hygiene are: cross-contamination; cleaning; chilling; cooking.

Cross-contamination

Bacteria spreading between food, surfaces or equipment causes cross-contamination. It is most likely to happen when raw food touches (or drips onto) ready-to-eat food, equipment or surfaces. It is one of the most common causes of food poisoning. To avoid it do the following:

- Thoroughly clean work surfaces, chopping boards and equipment before and after preparing food.

- Use different chopping boards and knives for raw and ready-to-eat food. You can even extend this further by using a red board for raw meat, blue for raw fish, green for raw vegetables and yellow for cooked food.

- Wash your hands before preparing food.

- Wash your hands thoroughly after touching raw food.

- Keep raw and ready-to-eat foods apart at all times.

- Store raw food below ready-to-eat food in the fridge.

- If possible, use separate fridges for raw and ready-to-eat food.

- Make sure that your staff know how to avoid cross-contamination.

Cleaning

Effective cleaning gets rid of bacteria on hands, surfaces and equipment. To stop harmful bacteria spreading on to food, do the following:

- Make sure that all your staff wash and dry their hands thoroughly before handling food.

- Clean food areas and equipment between different tasks, especially after handling raw food.

- Clear and clean as you go. Clear away used equipment, spilt food and so on as you work and clean all work surfaces thoroughly.

Chilling

Chilling food properly helps to stop harmful bacteria from growing. Some foods will need to be kept chilled to keep them safe, for example food with a 'use by' date, cooked dishes and other ready-to-eat food such as prepared salads and desserts. Don't leave these types of food standing around at room temperature. You can do the following:

- Check chilled food on delivery to make sure it is cold enough.

- Put food that needs to be kept chilled in the fridge straight away.

- Cool cooked food as quickly as possible and then put it in the fridge.

- Keep chilled food out of the fridge for the shortest time possible during preparation.

- Check regularly that your fridge and display units are cold enough.

Cooking

It is extremely important to make sure that food is cooked properly to kill any harmful bacteria. When cooking or reheating food, always check that it is piping hot all the way through.

It is especially important to make sure that you thoroughly cook poultry, rolled joints and products made from minced meat, such as burgers and sausages. This is because there could be bacteria present in the middle of these types of products. They should not be served pink or rare and should be piping hot all the way through. Whole cuts of meat (such as steaks) and whole joints of beef and lamb can be served pink or rare as long as they are fully sealed on the outside.

Temperature

You must not keep foods at temperatures that might cause a risk to health. The 'cold chain' must not be interrupted for those foods that rely on temperature control for their safety. However, you are allowed to have foods outside temperature control for limited periods of time to allow you to prepare, transport, store, display and serve food, as long as this does not cause a risk to health.

If foods are going to be kept or served at chilled temperatures, you must cool them as quickly as possible after cooking (or other heat processing), or after final preparation if you are not heating the foods, to a temperature that does not cause a risk to health. The temperature control requirements are as follows:

- Cold foods must be kept at 8°C or below. This is a legal requirement in England, Wales and Northern Ireland. In Scotland food must also be kept cold.

- Hot foods must be kept at 63°C or above. This is a legal requirement throughout the UK. When you reheat food, make sure that it is piping hot all the way through. In Scotland, there is a legal requirement for reheated foods to reach at least 82°C.

- When you are serving or displaying food, you can keep it out of temperature control for a limited period of time:
  - Cold foods can be kept above 8°C for up to four hours. You should only do this once. If any food is left after this time, you should throw it away or keep it chilled at 8°C or below until it is used.
  - Hot foods can be kept below 63°C for up to two hours. You should only do this once. If any food is left after this time, you should throw it away, reheat it to 63°C or above, or cool it as quickly as possible to 8°C or below.
  Remember to keep the food at a safe temperature until it is used.

Defrosting

If you defrost any foods you must do this in a way that minimises the risk of harmful bacteria growing, or toxins forming, in the foods. While they are being defrosted, you must keep foods at a temperature that will not result in a risk to health. Where liquid coming from the defrosting food may present a risk to health (for example, when defrosting raw meat) you must drain it off adequately. Following defrosting, food must be handled in a way that minimises the risk of harmful bacteria growing or toxins forming (for example, by keeping it in the fridge).

Stock rotation

Remember the rule first in, first out, to make sure that older food is used first. This will also help to prevent waste. When you put food in the fridge or storeroom, make sure the foods with a shorter use-by or best-before date are at the front of the shelf, in order that they are used first.

Food Alerts – a way of letting local authorities and consumers know about problems associated with food – are available through the FSA. You can register to receive automatic notifications via www.food.gov.uk/enforcement/alerts/ or have these sent to your mobile phone. To sign up for the free service, simply send the text message 'START FOOD' to 62372. To unsubscribe, text 'STOP FOOD' to the same number.

You can also check which foods are having to be withdrawn from the market by checking www.food.gov.uk/foodindustry/regulation/foodfeedform

Health and safety

You are responsible for the health and safety of your employees, visitors and customers. You must display a HSE Health and Safety notice if you have employees. If you have five employees or more, you must have a written health and safety policy (visit www.hse.gov.uk).

You must carry out a risk assessment of your workplace as well. Health is just as important as safety, so consider the noise levels, the lifting and carrying of objects and your smoking policies. You no longer have to hold a fire certificate but you must show you have carried out fire-risk assessments and have adequate controls in place. Further information can be obtained from your local Fire Safety Officer.

Licences

If you decide to sell alcohol, you must apply to your local authority for two licences. These are the premise licence and the personal licence. For the premise licence, the police and fire authorities will look very carefully at the application and satisfy themselves that you as the applicant and your premises are suitable for selling alcohol.

Holders of a personal licence require a recognised qualification, which includes knowledge of licensing laws. It's advisable to use the services of a specialist licensing professional to handle your application. Even though this will cost you in fees, it can speed up the process and help ensure that your application succeeds.

The Licensing Act regulates the sale of alcohol and the supply of hot food between the hours of 11 p.m. and 5 a.m. It is highly unlikely you will be open at these hours but that will depend on whether or not you decide to have a deli café as a complementary service.

Licences for the sale or supply of alcohol are dealt with by the local Environmental Health Department of your local council. If you plan to play background music in the shop you will also need to obtain licences from the Performing Right Society (PRS) at www.mcps-prs-alliance.co.uk, and from Phonographic Performance Limited (PPL) at www.ppluk.com – remember, there is an annual fee for these licences. Licensing laws can cause you some headaches intitally, but a good solicitor can usually sort out an application to obviate the most common problems.

Labelling

Some foods have labelling requirements that are just too complex to detail here and there are a number that deal specifically with eggs, honey, fish, beef, meat, jams, wine and chocolate products. Bill Drennan suggests:

For advice on the labelling of specific food products, we recommend that those setting up a deli business employ the services of a consultant or contact the Trading Standards department of your local county or unitary council, which have responsibility for food law enforcement. This includes the checking of product labels.

You can find the contact details of your local Trading Standards Office by visiting www.food.gov.uk/enforcement/laresource/yourarea. Alternatively, further information on labelling and copies of Agency Guidance notes can be found at www.food.gov.uk/foodindustry/guidancenotes/labelregsguidance

There are some exemptions under food labelling law for food which is displayed for sale in a loose or unwrapped state, or is sold from the same premises where it is pre-packed.

Environmental damage

Note that your business can be held responsible for any environmental damage it causes. Fines of more than £5,000 are common and there are no limits to financial penalties. Every business is legally responsible for the waste it produces. Advice is available from your local council and Defra (www.defra.gov.uk).

Refrigeration, air-conditioning and fire-fighting equipment can contain ozone-depleting substances. If your equipment contains CFCs, HCFCs or halons, you would be advised to call the Environment and Energy Helpline on 0800 585794.

Disability discrimination

If you intend employing someone, it is important to recognise how to avoid and prevent discrimination from occurring. This can be direct (where you openly treat someone less favourably than you may others) or indirect (where you might place an unnecessary condition or requirement on a particular job to prevent certain people from applying). The four Acts which focus on discrimination are:

☐ The Sex Discrimination Act 1975.

☐ The Equal Pay Act 1970.

☐ The Race Relations Act 1976.

☐ The Disability Discrimination Act 1995 (applying to companies with 15 or more employees).

With ten million people living in the UK with a disability who are covered by the Disability Discrimination Act 1995, it is essential you keep up to date with your obligations. The law firm Addleshaw Goddard recommends that retailers take note of a recent amendment to the Act. This extends the definition of disability to include mental illness, HIV, cancer and multiple sclerosis from the point of diagnosis and could mean a customer being entitled to bring a claim under the Act without you realising.

As an employer, it is unlawful for you to discriminate against a job applicant or an employee with one of these conditions and you must also make reasonable adjustments to your premises.

While the size of your shop and the resources available to you will determine what is a reasonable adjustment, it is important to be aware that you may have to look at various alterations such as widening doors, installing ramps and altering counter heights. See www.direct.gov.uk/en/DisabledPeople/index.htm and www.equalityhumanrights.com for further information.

Other details are also available from:

☐ The Office of Public Sector Information at www.opsi.gov.uk

☐ The Scottish Executive at www.scotland.gov.uk

☐ The Welsh Assembly Government at www.wales.gov.uk

☐ TheNorthern Ireland Executive at www.nothernireland.gov.uk

Rules about menus

If you sell take-away food or set up a deli café, there are rules concerning menus set out by the Food Standards Agency (FSA), as follows.

Displaying prices

When you sell food or drink for people to eat or drink on the premises, you must make the prices clear, for example on a price list or menu. You must include VAT in the prices when appropriate (see 'Charging VAT' below). If you add a service charge (a percentage or amount), or if there is a minimum charge, you must also display this with as much prominence as the other prices.

Charging VAT

Whether or not you need to include VAT in your prices, and what rate of VAT, depends on a number of different things. In general, businesses selling food or drink that is ready to eat or drink should charge VAT at the standard rate. But businesses that have a turnover (not just profit) below the 'registration threshold' do not need to be VAT registered, and therefore do not need to charge VAT (see 'VAT Explained', Chapter 5). If you become VAT registered, there are some rules that apply, for example, if you sell food or drink to be consumed on your premises, or if you supply hot take-away food, you must charge VAT at the standard rate on these products. Normally, you will not need to charge VAT on cold take-away food and drink, but there are some products where standard-rate VAT always applies, such as crisps, sweets and bottled water. Thus sometimes those caterers who supply food to a school or hospital do not have to charge VAT.

Describing food

You must always describe food and drink accurately on your menus, blackboards and adverts. Any illustrations must accurately represent the food you are selling. Descriptions and illustrations must not be misleading. Words like 'fresh', 'home-made' and 'suitable for vegetarians' can easily be used misleadingly.

Products described as 'sausages' or 'burgers' on menus must also contain a minimum amount of meat, by law. Contact your local authority for more information.

Labelling food

Usually, catering businesses will not have to label food. However, if it contains ingredients that have been irradiated, or are derived from genetically modified (GM) soya or maize, you must say this either on a label attached to the food, or on a menu, or on a notice that is easily visible to the customer.

The same rules apply to food that you pre-pack to sell direct to the customer (for example, sandwiches made and packed in advance in a sandwich bar). There are more extensive labelling rules for businesses that supply pre-packed food to catering or retail businesses, or that sell products for customers to cook at home. Once again, contact your local authority for more information.

10

BROADENING YOUR SCOPE

In addition to stocking a range of fine foods, you could also look at other ways of bringing in a regular income. You could even think about developing your own range of food with local producer partners: ice cream with dairy farmers; pies, pâtés and ready-made meals using local meat products; quiches made with local eggs. Your deli may become a meeting place as well as a locale for fine food products. Think about capitalising on this by offering café sales. According to The Guild of Fine Food's survey, 57% of sales come from take-away food and drink and eat-in accounts for 26% of sales on average.

Says Fi Buchanan, of Heart Buchanan Fine Food & Wine in Glasgow:

We are a community orientated shop where people come to meet. Two of our customers met here, got married and we catered for the wedding. Recently we catered for the christening of their first baby.

Take-away food sales

In addition to café sales, you can also offer a selection of take-away upmarket soups, salads, wraps, baked goods and sandwiches to local office workers. British consumers spent more than £5 billion on ready-made sandwiches from shops and foodservice outlets in the last 12 months, according to The British Sandwich Association (BSA). Furthermore, they spent more per sandwich than ever with the average price of a commercially made sandwich hitting a new high at £1.85. While ingredient prices, fuel and other inflationary factors look set to push the cost even higher, it seems that little is denting the consumer's appetite for sandwiches, with sales of Food on the Go products continuing to increase year-on-year.

The real challenge for the future, says the BSA, is whether the commercial sandwich market attracts consumers away from the lunchbox market, which in size matches that of the commercial sector. Accepting that this will not be an easy challenge – as 'consumers do not think it costs anything to make a sandwich at home' – the report suggests that the industry, and retailers in particular, need to focus more closely on the lunchbox market as a category in its own right. One of the concerns for the commercial sandwich market is the increasing pressure being placed on manufacturers of packaged sandwiches to meet government health guidelines, particularly in relation to salt levels, against growing evidence that consumers are rejecting the advice on this issue.

The BSA report also looked at ingredients and revealed that the wrap bubble may have finally reached its limit, with sales down in the Food on the Go market by 1% in volume over the last year. By contrast bagel sales have grown by some 66% – albeit off a low base. They now account for about 1% of sandwich sales. Wraps by comparison account for 3%. The traditional triangular sandwich continues to hold its own. In the last year it outstripped overall market growth by almost 2% and now accounts for nearly 67% of all sandwich sales.

In terms of fillings, chicken continues to dominate the sandwich market. Last year the association estimated that some 39,700 tonnes of chicken meat went into sandwiches compared to 8,250 tonnes of ham and 6,500 tonnes of cheese. However, you can build sandwich sales by adding zippy condiments, creating signature sandwiches, satisfying gourmet tastes with speciality cheeses and meats, offering healthy options, varying the veggies and toppings and by serving hot sandwiches.

Joining the British Sandwich Association (www.sandwich.org.uk) as a retail member costs £135 plus VAT per year. Otherwise you can subscribe to the official magazine, *International Sandwich & Snack News*, and also have access to advisory services for £55.

Niche markets and special events

A healthy lunchbox service to schools in your area or smoothies, fitness shakes and other health food items to health-conscious customers are other possibilities. The combination of healthy food, tasty food and fast food can definitely work. There are tremendous opportunities to sell seasonal lines as well: Valentine's Day, Mother's Day, Easter, Father's Day, Halloween, Bonfire Night and Christmas all offer chances to sell themed products. Speciality foods always make great gift items, so put together a range of interesting and appropriate products. Hampers containing a selection of good food and wines are ideal. Regional food hampers for visitors at local tourist attractions will place your deli on the national epicurean highway. Consumers will also want to offer their guests an assortment of wonderful foods and lunch or dinner parties.

Picnic hampers are a must during the summer. The history of the picnic dates back to the 14th century when medieval feasts were held outside before hunting. The name comes from the French *piquenique*, an informal meal eaten in the open air. The foods were mainly hams, baked meats and pastries. The Great British Picnic has come a long way since then and you could build hampers with such delights as regional sausages, cold roasts, speciality loaves, mustard, horseradish, local Chapel Down and High Cup wines, and a selection of some of the 700 cheeses produced in Britain.

Sponsoring a local event is another way of promoting your deli positively within the community and local papers are also usually happy to cover stories about businesspeople who are actively contributing to the community.

Take your gourmet deli on the road and offer your speciality delights to businesses, college campuses and the like. You'll find hungry customers who want a good meal but don't have the time to either drive to a restaurant or sit down for lunch. Lunch platters can also be made up with a mixture of sandwiches, falafel or other snacks and delivered to businesses in the area. Alternatively, you could supply freshly prepared evening meals for reheating to those on their way home from work.

Don't overlook the possibility of supplying the catering trade, particularly if your area has eateries which offer continental cuisine. For example, if you plan to offer a wide range of Italian fine foods and wines you could call on local Italian restaurants to see if they would be interested in ordering on a regualr basis. Perhaps you propose to make up some dishes yourself, such as pâtés. You could bring a few samples along to show the quality of your products to prospective trade customers. If you are based at the seaside or near a port, yacht catering is another option.

You may decide to offer a discount to your customers as a matter of course. For example, you could reduce the price of anything nearing its best-before or use-by date, or discount small pieces of salami, ends of hams, smoked salmon trimmings and so on. As part of a promotion you might offer a discount on a related item, provided a full-price product is bought at the same time. For example, half-price vinegar with every bottle of olive oil.

So now that you've read this far what are you waiting for? Whatever you end up doing, do it with passion and love.

Go for it – and good luck!

TRADE PUBLICATIONS AND WEBSITES

Convenience Store (www.convenience-store.co.uk), William Reed Business Media, fortnightly, £65 per year.

Deli Business (www.delibusiness.com), US-based magazine, Phoenix Media, alternate monthly, $79.70 per year.

Fine Food Digest (www.finefoodworld.co.uk), The Guild of Fine Food, published ten times a year, costs £40 per year.

Food Manufacture (www.foodmanufacture.co.uk), William Reed Business Media, monthly, £81 per year.

The Grocer (www.thegrocer.co.uk), William Reed Business Media, monthly, £95 per year.

Independent Retail News (www.talkingretail.com), Nexus Business Media, fortnightly, £115 per year.

International Sandwich & Snack News, The British Sandwich Association, eight times a year, £55 per year.

The Retailer Magazine (www.brc.org.uk), British Retail Consortium, six times a year, £30 per year.

Speciality Food (www.specialityfoodmagazine.com), Aceville Publications, £25 per year.

Talking Retail (www.talkingretail.com), is an online trade publication and a useful source of free information and leaflets.

USEFUL ORGANISATIONS

Acas (Advisory, Conciliation & Arbitration Service), Brandon House, 180 Borough High Street, London SE1 1LW. Tel: 020-7210 3613; helpline 0845-747 4747; www.acas.org.uk and 13 regional offices.

Association of British Insurers (ABI), 51 Gresham Street, London EC2V 7HQ. Tel: 020-7600 3333; www.abi.org.uk

Association of Chartered Accountants (ACCA), 29 Lincoln's Inn Fields, London WC2A 3EE. Tel: 020-7059 5000; email info@accaglobal.com; www.accaglobal.com

The British Chamber of Commerce (BCC) is an association of the main Chambers of Commerce found in each region of the UK. Each chamber is a separate membership organisation and the services provided can vary with each Chamber. Businesses of all sizes may join their local Chamber on payment of the relevant annual membership fee. A list of Chambers can be obtained from the BCC, 65 Petty France, London SW1H 9EU. Tel: 020-7654 5800; email info@britishchambers.org.uk; www.britishchambers.org.uk

British Franchise Association, A2 Danebrook Court, Oxford Office Village, Langford Lane, Oxford OX5 1LQ. Tel: 01865-379892; www.thebfa.org

British Frozen Food Federation, 3rd Floor, Springfield House, Springfield Business Park, Springfield Road, Grantham, Lincolnshire NG31 7BG. Tel: 01476-515300; email generaladmin@bff.co.uk; www.bff.co.uk

British Insurance Brokers' Association, 14 Bevis Marks, London EC3A 7NT. Tel: 0870-950 1790; email enquiries@biba.org.uk; www.biba.org.uk

British Retail Consortium, 21 Dartmouth Street, London SW1H 9BP. Tel: 020-7854 8900; www.brc.org.uk is the lead trade association representing the whole range of retailers, including independents, and selling a wide range of products through centre of town, out of town, rural and virtual stores.

The British Sandwich Association, Association House, 18c Moor Street, Chepstow NP16 5DB. Tel: 01291-628103; www.sandwich.org.uk

Buying Support Agency, Montpellier House, 14 Granley Road, Cheltenham, Gloucestershire GL51 6LG. Tel: 0845-555 3344; www.buyingsupport.co.uk

Carbon Trust, 8th Floor, 3 Clement's Inn, London WC2A 2AZ. Tel: 0800-085 2005; www.carbontrust.co.uk

Chartered Institute of Marketing, Moor Hall, Cookham, Maidenhead, Berkshire SL6 9QH. Tel: 01628-427500; www.cim.co.uk

Chilled Food Association, PO Box 6434, Kettering, Northhampstonshire NN15 5AF. Tel: 01536-515395; email cfa@chilledfood.org; www.chilledfood.org

City & Guilds, 1 Giltspur Street, London EC1A 9DD. Tel: 020-7294 2800; email leanersupport@cityandguilds.com; www.cityandguilds.com

Companies House, Crown Way, Cardiff CF14 3UZ. Tel: 0870-333 3636; www.companieshouse.gov.uk

Confederation of British Industry (CBI), 103 New Oxford Street, London WC1A 1DU. Tel: 020-7379 7400; www.cbi.org.uk

Defra (Department for Environment, Food and Rural Affairs), CCU 7th Floor, Eastbury House, 30–34 Albert Embankment, London SE1 7TL; www.defra.gov.uk has Food Industry Hub teams which work together with the food sector, including retailers, food service, manufacturers and wholesalers. The Hub also acts as the first point of contact and advisory point within the organisation on assured food standards.

Department for Business, Enterprise & Regulatory Reform (BERR), 1 Victoria Street, London SW1H 0ET. Tel: 020-7215 5000; email enquiries@berr.gsi.gov.uk; www.berr.gov.uk

Fairtrade Foundation, Room 204, 16 Baldwin's Gardens, London EC1N 7RJ; www.fairtrade.org.uk is part of the international Fairtrade movement and oversees all aspects of Fairtrade in the UK – including retailing.

Federation of Small Businesses (FSB), Sir Frank Whittle Way, Blackpool Business Park, Blackpool FY4 2FE. Tel: 01253-336000; email ho@fsb.co.uk; www.fsb.co.uk

Finance and Leasing Association (FLA), 2nd Floor, Imperial House, 15–19 Kingsway, London WC2B 6UN. Tel: 020-7836 6511; email info@fla.org.uk, www.fla.org.uk

Financial Ombudsman Service (FOS), South Quay Plaza, 183 Marsh Wall, London E14 9SR. Tel: 0845-080 1800; www.financial-ombudsman.org.uk

Financial Services Authority (FSA), 25 The North Colonnade, Canary Wharf, London E14 5HS. Tel: 020-7066 1000; helpline 0845-606 1234; www.fsa.gov.uk

The Food and Drink Federation, 6 Catherine Street, London WC2B 5JJ. Tel: 020-7836 2460; www.fdf.org.uk is the trade association for the food and drink manufacturing industry. It works on behalf of members to support them on trade and policy issues. Affiliate membership is open to trade associations and companies which are not food and drink manufacturers but which have an interest in the food and drink manufacturing industry. The annual fixed rate fee is £1,100. The Scottish Food and Drink Federation (SFDF) is at 4a Torphichen Street, Edinburgh EH3 8JQ. Tel: 0131-229 9415; www.sfdf.org.uk

The Food Standards Agency, Aviation House, 125 Kingsway, London WC2B 6NH. Tel: 020-7276 8000; www.food.gov.uk is an independent watchdog that was set up to regulate food businesses and protect public health.

Forum of Private Business, Ruskin Chambers, Drury Lane, Knutsford WA16 6HA. Tel: 01565-634467; email info@fpb.org; www.fpb.co.uk

Franchise Development Services (FDS), Franchise House, 56 Surrey Street, Norwich NR1 3FD. Tel: 01603-620301; email enquiries@fdsltd.com; www.fdsfranchise.com

The Guild of Fine Food, Guild House, Station Road, Wincanton, Somerset BA9 9FE. Tel: 01963-824464; www.finefoodworld.co.uk is a UK trade association for anyone making or selling top quality local, regional and speciality food and drink. The Guild helps fine food shops compete against the power of supermarkets. Through its Accredited Supplier system, it helps specialist retailers identify and stock thousands of exceptional products that cannot be found in the larger supermarkets.

Health and Safety Executive, Rose Court, 2 Southwark Bridge, London SE1 9HS. Tel: 0845-345 0055; www.hse.gov.uk

ICS Ltd, Clydeway Centre, Skypark 5, 1st Floor, 45 Finnieston Street, Glasgow G3 8JU. Tel: 0141-302 5487; email icscourseadvisors@ics-uk.co.uk; www.icslearn.co.uk

The Institute of Chartered Accountants in England and Wales (ICAEW), PO Box 433, Chartered Accountants Hall, Moorgate Place, London EC2P 2BJ. Tel: 020-7920 8100; www.icaew.co.uk

The Institute of Chartered Accounts of Scotland (ICAS), CA House, 21 Haymarket Yards, Edinburgh EH12 5BH. Tel: 0131-347 0100; www.icas.org.uk

Institute of Grocery Distribution (IGD), Grange Lane, Letchmore Heath, Watford, Hertfordshire WD25 8GD. Tel: 01923-857141; email igd@igd.com; www.igd.com produces a vast range of publications covering all aspects of the UK's food and grocery industry.

Institute of Insurance Brokers (IIB), Higham Business Centre, Midland Road, Higham Ferrers, Northamptonshire NN10 8DW. Tel: 01933-410003; www.iib-uk.com

The Law Society, 113 Chancery Lane, London WC2A 1PL, to find a solicitor. Tel: 0870-606 2555; www.lawsociety.org.uk

learndirect, Dearing House, Young Street, Sheffield S1 4UP. Tel: 0800-101 901; www.learndirect.co.uk

National Federation of Enterprise Agencies (NFEA), 12 Stephenson Court, Fraser Road, Priory Business Park, Bedford MK44 3WJ. Tel: 01234-831623; email enquiries@nfea.com; www.nfea.com a membership body for Local Enterprise Agencies, offers a comprehensive range of services to pre-start, start-up and micro businesses. It also runs the Small Business Advice Service (SBAS) at www.smallbusinessadvice.org.uk which provides an internet-based advice service for entrepreneurs, owner managers and the self-employed.

Office for National Statistics, Cardiff Road, Newport NP10 8XG.
Tel: 0845-601 3034; www.statistics.gov.uk

OU Business School, The Open University, Walton Hall, Milton Keynes MK7 6AA.
Tel: 01908-655888; email general-enquiries@open.ac.uk; www.open.ac.uk/oubs

Prince's Initiative for Mature Enterprise (PRIME), Astral House, 1268 London Road, London SW16 4ER. Tel: 020-8765 7833; email prime@ace.org.uk; www.primeinitiative.org.uk

The Prince's Trust, 18 Park Square East, London NW1 4LH. Tel: 020-7543 1234; www.princes-trust.org.uk

The Royal Institute of Public Health, 28 Portland Place, London W1B 1DE.
Tel: 020-7291 8366; www.riph.org.uk

Shell Livewire, Hawthorn House, Forth Banks, Newcastle-upon-Tyne NE1 5JG.
Tel: 0191-261 5584; www.shell-livewire.org

The Small Business Bureau, Curzon House, Church Road, Windlesham, Surrey GU20 6BH. Tel: 01276-452010; www.smallbusinessbureau.org.uk is a voice for the SME sector. It costs £58.75 to join, which includes a copy of *Small Business News* (three times a year). The organisation also holds an annual conference which is said to be 'the largest SME event outside the USA.'

The Soil Association, South Plaza, Marlborough Street, Bristol BS1 3NX.
Tel: 0117-314 5000; www.soilassociation.org promotes organic food, farming and forestry. The Soil Association Scotland can be found at 18 Liberton Brae, Tower Mains, Edinburgh EH16 6AE. Tel: 0131-666 2474; email contact@sascotland.org

Valuation Office Agency (VOA), New Court, 48 Carey Street, London WC2A 2JE.
Tel: 020-7506 1700 (or 0845 602 1507 goes directly to the office closest to you); www.voa.gov.uk

Wenta Business Services. Tel: 0845-371 0891; email admin@wenta.co.uk; www.wenta.co.uk. Offices in Bedford, Borehamwood, Hemel Hempstead, Luton, Potters Bar and Watford.

WiRE (Women in Rural Enterprise), Harper Adams University College, Edgmond, Newport, Shropshire TF10 8NB. Tel: 01952-815338; email info@wireuk.org; www.wireuk.org offers business support to women in rural business.

WRAP, The Old Academy, 21 Horse Fair, Banbury, Oxford OX16 0AH.
Tel: 01295-819900; helpline 0808 100 2040; email helpline@wrap.org.uk; www.wrap.org.uk

See also:

Business Link (England)
Tel: 0845-600 9006
www.businesslink.gov.uk

Flexible Support for Business (Wales)
Tel: 0300-060 3000
www.business-support-wales.gov.uk

Business Gateway (Scotland)
Tel: 0845-609 6611
www.bgateway.com

Scottish Enterprise
Tel: 0845-607 8787
www.scottish-enterprise.com

Invest Northern Ireland
Tel: 028-9023 9090
www.investni.com

HM Revenue & Customs
Tel: 0845-915 4515
www.hmrc.gov.uk

INDEX